Jane Hurshman-Corkum
Life and Death after Billy

Vernon L.Oickle

NIMBUS
PUBLISHING

Nimbus Publishing Limited
P.O. Box 9301, Station A
Halifax, N.S. B3K 5N5
(902) 455-4286

Design: Arthur B. Carter, Halifax
Printed and bound in Canada

Canadian Cataloguing in Publication Data

Oickle, Vernon L.

Life and death after Billy
ISBN 1-55109-035-X

1. Stafford, Jane, 1949-1992. 2. Abused wives—
Nova Scotia—Biography. I. Title.

HV6626.052 1993   362.82'92'092   C93-098502-8

Dedicated to
the memory of
Jane Hurshman-Corkum

I've been to hell, touched it, felt it and came back again.
Jane Hurshman-Corkum

Contents

Acknowledgements

There are certain people I must thank and acknowledge for their guidance in making this book a reality.

First and foremost, I must thank Jane herself for the inspiration she provided. In the ten years I knew her, I was fortunate to be able to call her a friend. It is because of that friendship that I have written this book. It is the result of many interviews, personal conversations and media accounts about the life of Jane Hurshman-Corkum and it is dedicated to her memory. While the text is based on fact, the names of some individuals have been altered for their protection while others are composite characters to represent a specific mood or incident.

During the years following her trial, I maintained an extensive file on Jane Hurshman, from which I drew information for this book. It is appropriate then, that I gratefully acknowledge these sources: *The Liverpool Advance*, *The Yarmouth Vanguard*, *The Daily News*, *The Chronicle-Herald*, *The Globe and Mail*, *Chatelaine*, and CBC Television.

Additionally, I would be remiss if I did not thank the family and friends of Jane Hurshman who so willingly spoke with me. Most notably, a special thanks to Rev. Margie Whynot and Ann Keith whose cooperation and words of encouragement were greatly appreciated. Thanks as well to Maurice Hurshman, the Cole Harbour RCMP Detachment, and the Halifax City Police.

Writing a book is no easy task and often requires the assistance of others. With that in mind, I must acknowledge the efforts of Brian Freeman and Rachael Smith for their roles in making this project a reality. As well, I am grateful to Dorothy Blythe at Nimbus Publishing for giving this book the nod and to Dean Jobb for his insightful and thorough critique.

There were times when writing this book that my personal life had to suffer. Therefore, I am particularly grateful for my wife Nancy who so willing gave me the support and encouragement I needed during those long months.

However, it was my young son who provided me with the real inspiration to write this book. All children should be allowed to experience childhood without the fear and horror of abuse. It is my hope that this book will spread Jane's message of hope and survival.

Vernon L. Oickle

Introduction

In the fall of 1991, Jane Hurshman said to me, "Right now, there is a man out there somewhere beating his wife or girlfriend.... I know that woman; she was me only a few years ago. I know her pain and her suffering. I know how much she wants to get away from that madman and I would help her if I could. Maybe my story will help to let her know she isn't alone and to show her there can be a good life out there. I am only one voice, but I hope I can make a difference for this woman and thousands of others like her."

I remember the first time I heard the name Jane (Stafford) Hurshman. It was the fall of 1982. Only months earlier, I had graduated from journalism school and was eager to begin a career in the newspaper business. I was fortunate to find a job with my hometown newspaper, *The Advance*, immediately upon graduation.

As a small-town community newspaper, resources were very limited but I was still surprised and a bit overwhelmed when my editor, Jock Inglis, assigned me to cover the first-degree murder trial of Jane (Stafford) Hurshman. It was through Jane's trial that I first learned about the tragedy of domestic violence and abuse.

Even after ten years, I can still vividly recall my feelings while covering this sensational trial. I remember returning to the office at the end of each court day and being emotionally and physically wiped out. I may have been somewhat naive, but coming to grips with the horror story that was unfolding was difficult to deal with. Hearing about the pain and suffering that one man had inflicted upon his wife and children seemed to be too much for me to accept, let alone write about.

Like many other people in the community, I wanted to dismiss the accounts of abuse as mere fiction, but through the course of the trial, it became clear that Jane's pain was real and her common-law husband, Billy Stafford, had been a madman. Her story was not only an eye-opener for myself but for the community as a whole; we were horrified to learn of the suffering this woman and her children had endured at the hands of Billy Stafford. Prior to the trial there was little talk about wife abuse in Queens County, but soon Jane's trial would become the focus of national attention. Her story opened the floodgates in the small community and gave momentum to a cause that had been virtually nonexistent — Jane was eventually to become a national symbol of hope and strength for thousands of abuse victims.

Before the 1980s, awareness of domestic violence and the deep-rooted, long-lasting suffering it caused was very limited. Society kept the hideous secret hidden from even the most discerning eye, destroying countless lives of women and children in the process. The many victims of wife and child abuse have endured such irreparable damage that even time cannot heal the wounds. Today, these individuals struggle for some sort of normal existence.

Silence was the order of the day as the truth remained buried beneath an almost unpenetrable veil of lies and deception. Women, it was widely believed, were the property of their husbands or partners and whatever happened in their home was secret. Unfortunately, despite all the progress that has been made in recent years through the tireless efforts of abuse survivors, advocacy groups, and government agencies, the silence is still deafening, serving to protect those who destroy one of society's most sacred institutions, the family. Abusers care little that the family unit should be one of love and trust. Instead, they submerge their victims in a sea of pain and suffering that will never end even when, or if, the abuse stops.

There are those who will never believe that a husband and father who beats up his wife and children is abusive, regarding this as an acceptable form of discipline. And there are those who will continue to believe that what goes on behind the closed doors of their neighbour's home is best left there. As well, others will maintain that any woman who stays in an abusive relationship must "like what she gets" or "asked" for it. It is obvious that no amount of public education will ever change this line of reasoning. Regardless of how many victims come forward to tell their stories, there will always be a certain faction of society who will never sympathize.

In part, much of this denial comes from guilt associated with the knowledge that, indirectly, society condones this abuse by its inaction, complacency, and traditional beliefs. From early childhood, males are taught to be the dominant force in society while women are made to feel less than equal. Even the simplest tradition, such as the father giving the bride away to another man during a wedding ceremony, ingrains the learned belief that females are meant to be the property of men. It is no surprise then that, by turning our collective backs to the truth, society sends a message to the abuser that we will not interfere and that although outwardly we may not condone their actions we will do nothing to stop them.

In recent years there has been some progress. For instance, on the South Shore of Nova Scotia, some headway has been made during the past decade. In January 1983, the Second Story Women's Centre, a resource/drop-in centre for women, opened its doors in Bridgewater. Within a few months, it became obvious that women in crisis needed help. A grass-roots group of concerned citizens eventually evolved under the auspices of the women's centre, and by year's end began to offer a twenty-four-hour emergency service to women in crisis along the South Shore.

A local helpline, another residual spin-off agency that today continues to operate an emergency service, was established in Bridgewater in January 1984. This service refers calls from battered women to support groups and/or community services. Shortly after these helplines were established, it soon became apparent that a shelter for battered women was needed on the South Shore as victims wanting to leave their abusive relationships were forced to find sanctuary at a Halifax transition house or some other facility approved by government agencies.

Finally, in the mid-1980s, a local initiative was launched to establish a regional transition house on the South Shore. Although it was a major challenge for those involved, Harbour House was opened in Bridgewater and today it continues to provide a safe haven for hundreds of battered women and their children from Queens and Lunenburg Counties. Statistics confirm the facility meets a growing need. In 1991-92, Harbour House served in excess of one hundred and fifty clients.

Before these safety nets were available, abused women were trapped in their domestic prisons and left with few alternatives for escape. For a woman with children, little financial power and no self-esteem, the fear and anger can be overwhelming. It was for that reason that on March 11, 1982, Jane (Stafford) Hurshman took the law into her own hands and shot her tormentor to death.

Jane confessed to killing Billy Stafford, who for five years had forced she and her children to endure countless acts of physical and emotional torture. She stood trial on a charge of first-degree murder and was ultimately found not guilty by a jury of her peers. Those are the facts. However, while some people agree that Jane had already done her time while living with Billy Stafford, others insist that she got away with murder. What they choose to forget is the fact that Jane's lawyer, Alan Ferrier, did not ask the jury to set her free. Instead, the defense urged the eleven men and women of the jury to find her guilty of a lesser charge; manslaughter.

In the course of deliberations, the jury found Jane (Stafford) Hurshman not guilty. Some find that difficult to accept, but others continue to applaud the outcome of the first trial, which has become a benchmark in Canadian law because it marked the first time the battered wife syndrome was used successfully as a defence. However, the Crown appealed the jury's verdict and a new trial was ordered. Jane then pleaded guilty to manslaughter, was sentenced to six months in prison and did her time. From that point on, she tried to build a normal life for herself and her children, at the same time continuing to be a highly visible and vocal opponent of domestic violence.

During the course of those legal proceedings, I got to know Jane very well and considered her a friend, not because she stood for anything in particular or because she had become a hero in the women's movement, but because I found her to be kind and considerate and because she always seemed to care about other people. Even during her ordeal, she worried about her children, her parents, and even the family of Billy Stafford. She held no grudges, but instead offered to help those who needed her the most—other victims of domestic violence.

She was not a woman who sought public attention. Instead, she was thrust into the limelight through circumstances over which she had little control. She did not ask to be abused and tortured. She readily admitted to killing Billy Stafford and continued to suffer even after his death. It is true Jane Hurshman became a champion in the women's rights

movement, but not out of a desire to become a celebrity. She wanted to
help others who were trapped in similar situations and she believed that
her words might actually give other abused women the courage to carry
on.

In light of her premature death in late February 1992, we will never
know about Jane's private pain. However, it goes without saying that
she suffered a great deal. I believe an editorial I wrote following her
death sums up how I felt about the woman I called a friend.

> *Jane Hurshman-Corkum.*
>   *The name means many things to different people. To her*
> *family, she was a troubled but loving wife and daughter, as*
> *well as a caring mother and sister. To her co-workers, she*
> *was a dedicated employee who was dependable and reliable.*
> *To her friends, she was a thoughtful person who wanted to*
> *ease the suffering of others.*
>   *But to the world, Jane Hurshman-Corkum was a vocal*
> *and undaunted opponent of wife abuse. In recent years, her*
> *name became synonymous with the issues of domestic vio-*
> *lence, a public lifestyle that surely brought with it a personal*
> *stress that others cannot imagine.*
>   *For the people of Queens County, the name Jane*
> *Hurshman-Corkum has its own meaning. Following the*
> *recent news of her death, the many questions and theories*
> *that surrounded the killing of Billy Stafford ten years ago*
> *surfaced again. However, whatever you think happened in*
> *March 1982 when Billy Stafford died may have little bearing*
> *on the events which led up to the death of Jane Hurshman-*
> *Corkum on the weekend of February 21, 1992.*
>   *Likewise, whether you believe Billy Stafford was abusive*
> *is a moot point now in light of the events of recent weeks.*
> *During the sensational and highly-publicized trials of Jane*
> *(Stafford) Hurshman, the defence painted an ugly picture of*
> *a man who pushed the limits of domestic violence to the*
> *extreme. You can believe the testimony or not. However, a*
> *jury found her innocent of first-degree murder and that's a*
> *fact.*
>   *In the years that followed her trials and period of incar-*

ceration in the wake of the Crown's appeal, Jane (Stafford) Hurshman became a vocal opponent of wife abuse. She lived a public life of constant exposure and was not allowed to forget her painful past. She believed that only by speaking out would the cycle of domestic violence be broken and, because of that belief, she shared her life over and over again, despite the personal toll it may have been taking.

However, while some saw only the public side of Jane (Stafford) Hurshman, the people close to her knew that in reality her personal suffering continued and in the end perhaps that private pain caught up to her, becoming too much to bear. There are many questions about her death, some of which may never be answered, but suffice it to say her life made a difference.

Despite the public appearances, the book Life With Billy and a soon-to-be-made movie based on that book, Jane Hurshman-Corkum was basically a private person who put on a brave front. In an interview with The Advance only weeks before her death, she told us the only reason she continued with the public lifestyle was to set an example for other abused women. She believed her message was important: women are being abused and silence is their worst enemy.

As well, she knew some people would be critical of her continued efforts to bring attention to the issue of wife abuse and she knew some would condemn the movie project. However, she believed issues such as domestic abuse need as much media attention as possible. Some may say she liked the attention, but others point out she felt obligated to speak out about the issues because of her own pain and suffering.

Despite the fact that Jane Hurshman-Corkum gained considerable notoriety since the death of Billy Stafford, she always insisted she did not like being considered a celebrity and that it was her message which was important.

A quote from the interview I had with Jane explains how she felt about her celebrity status. "That's a hard thing to live up to. It doesn't give you any room to be human; it doesn't give you any chance to fall down once in awhile. It's really *not fair that people put you on a pedestal. Sometimes, I feel like I'm under a microscope."* Jane Hurshman-Corkum *would be the first to point out she wasn't perfect nor was she a hero. But despite her feelings and the personal toll it was taking, she continued to speak out against domestic violence.*

Jane was a woman of great courage despite her personal turmoil and she felt she had a story to tell. It is my hope that this book will amplify her message and do justice to her memory.

Prologue

Inside a snug bungalow in the Halifax suburb of Cole Harbour, on a dull February afternoon, a dark-haired, forty-three-year-old woman went peacefully about her chores. Nothing seemed out of the ordinary. It was the same routine she had followed for the past eight years. Working the nightshift as a nursing assistant meant she slept until noon. When she got up, she had the rest of the day to do housework and attend whatever meetings or functions she had scheduled. Today, however, there were no meetings so she spent the time at home. She and her new husband had just recently moved into the house and she felt comfortable there.

Her day consisted of housework and preparing a meal for the eventual return of her sons later in the afternoon. Earlier that day her husband had driven to Queens County to visit with her parents. He would be gone overnight, but the boys would enjoy a good home-cooked meal.

After cleaning the house, the phone calls began. These were not frivolous calls for this was a woman on a mission. Usually they were to other women in trouble with the law or to women who were trapped in an abusive relationship and needed to hear a friendly voice. In recent years these calls had become more frequent and she understood the need these women had for a sounding board. In fact, she gave of herself so much that at times it hurt. Yet she had no desire to stop; she felt compelled to extend a helping hand.

But not all of the phone calls that day were of this nature; one was with a close friend. This was a strange conversation where she expressed fears that the phone in her home may have been tapped. Cautiously, she told her friend that she felt someone was listening in on their conversation and they would have to keep it short.

Later she chatted with her son's girlfriend, who had come by the house for a visit. After supper the dishes were washed and put away and it was time to head into the city. Before her work shift started at 11 o'clock she had plans to meet someone. On her way, she stopped at a Dartmouth mall to buy a birthday cake.

Jane Hurshman-Corkum left the safety of her Cole Harbour home at 8 p.m. on February 21, 1992. It would be the last time her family saw her alive.

At some point, between that time and 3:15 p.m. on Sunday, February 23, a single bullet fired from an old .38 calibre revolver took her life. Reaction to her death was immediate—police said it was suicide; family and friends said it was murder. Today, the mystery remains.

Only weeks prior to her death, Cole Harbour RCMP and the Halifax Police Department confirm that Jane had been receiving threatening messages and phone calls telling her to "shut up" about wife abuse or she would "be shut up." She first reported the threats to the RCMP on January 6. In fact, only a few days before her death, Jane had made arrangements to meet with police to discuss the threats. She was concerned that because she had a prison record, authorities would not take her report seriously. Police say she was mistaken in this as such threats are always considered legitimate and are carefully investigated.

Jane received five death threats over a six-week period—two written and three by telephone. Friends and family say the contents of the messages terrified Jane to the extent that only weeks before her death she had been attempting to purchase a gun that she claimed she wanted for her own protection. The two written threats and a recording of one of the phone calls are presently in the hands of the Cole Harbour RCMP and their crime laboratories in Ottawa. Although Halifax City Police have now closed their file on Jane's death, ruling it a suicide, the RCMP are continuing to probe the threats. Yet it could be as late as mid-1993 before results of their investigations are known.

Authorities explain that whoever sent the written messages used stencils, leaving no traceable handwriting. One telephone threat was recorded on an answering machine at the offices of the Elizabeth Fry

Society, an advocacy agency based in the Halifax-Dartmouth area with a mandate to assist women in trouble with the law. This taped threat is being carefully scrutinized as it was mechanically distorted to disguise the caller's voice. Those who have heard the recording say the voice has been altered and there is no way to identify the caller. In fact, Cole Harbour RCMP confirm the distortion is so extreme it is even difficult to determine whether the caller was a male or female.

Jane was a member of the Elizabeth Fry Society's board of directors and worked closely for more than a year with Elizabeth Forestell, the organization's executive director. Forestell recalls the day that she intercepted the message telling Jane to "shut up or be shut up." She says there is no way to identify the caller because it was impossible to say if the caller that left the threat was male or female, old or young, or if they were calling long distance or from within the city.

During the investigation into her death, police theorized that perhaps Jane had sent herself the threats to make her suicide look like a murder. Her family and friends, however, take the threats seriously and question what she would have gained from such a macabre plot. Family members also wonder about the effort that went into investigating Jane's death and say the police had already predetermined she had committed suicide before the investigation was complete. Should the police not have maintained an open mind until all the facts were known, they ask? They wonder if the authorities overlooked important clues that may have supported a murder theory because they had already made up their minds that Jane had killed herself.

Two days after she left for work, the body of Jane Hurshman-Corkum was discovered in her four-door, dark-blue Ford sedan by a pedestrian at approximately 3:15 p.m. The vehicle had been parked in a Lower Water Street lot near the Brewery Market on the Halifax waterfront.

What happened to Jane that weekend when she left the safety of her Cole Harbour home? There are many theories, but more questions.

Authorities confirm when Jane left her home on the evening of February 21, she had told her son's girlfriend she had plans to meet someone before going to work because her shift at the Halifax County Regional Rehabilitation Centre, where she was employed as a certified nursing assistant, was not scheduled to begin until 11 p.m. When Jane failed to show up for work, she was reported missing at around 1 a.m. on the morning of Saturday, February 22.

Who was Jane meeting before going to work? Police wonder that if, indeed, there was an actual meeting, could this person provide some answers that might unlock the mysteries surrounding the woman's death. On the other hand, police have also stated they are not convinced that a meeting ever took place but speculate instead that Jane planted the story of a supposed rendezvous with a mysterious person to further her suicide-made-to-look-like-a-murder plan.

Police officials point out they uncovered no evidence to indicate Jane's death was anything but a suicide. They point to the fact that in 1989, Jane had attempted suicide by taking a pill overdose and she was known by many of her friends and family to be suicidal. As well, they reason, Jane had admitted to a close friend in a letter not long before her death that she would rather be dead than face an upcoming court appearance on shoplifting charges.

Jane had been in trouble with the law on many occasions throughout the years for shoplifting, charges which doctors said resulted from kleptomania. In support of their suicide theory, authorities speculate Jane killed herself instead of going to court because she did not want to be an embarrassment to her family and friends. They further theorize that Jane committed suicide but tried to make it look like murder to shelter her family from the truth. Her suicide/murder scheme became more plausible and gained more credence when she added the death threats and possible telephone tap to the plot.

These are the facts according to the Halifax City Police Department: Jane's body was found in a position which indicated there was no second person in the vehicle; there was no sign of a struggle; the old .38 calibre revolver that fired the fatal bullet was found in the car; the bullet itself was trapped in the upholstery of the front seat directly behind where Jane was sitting; and the location of the handgun on the floor near the front driver's side door was consistent with the theory that she dropped the weapon once it was discharged. Furthermore, despite a light dusting of snow that had fallen in the metro area on that cold winter weekend, there were no footprints around the vehicle to indicate someone had exited the car once it was parked in the lot. Police explain even if footprints had been covered by fresh snow, depressions in the old snow would still have been detected, but none were discovered.

Investigators say there were no suspicious fingerprints found in the vehicle or on the gun. Authorities also confirm there was no serial number on the gun, indicating it was an early model made before numbers were required. For that reason, the gun's owner may never be identified. Police say that although there were no guns registered in Jane's name, they do know from her husband that she was in possession of a handgun only a few months before her death, but, they add, they are not sure if it was the same weapon used to take her life.

Authorities say they do have collaborating evidence which supports their belief the gun belonged to Jane. In the vehicle, police discovered a blanket on the back seat in which they believe the gun may have been concealed. They now speculate, based on forensic tests, that Jane used the blanket to muffle the gunshot and mask the flash in the dark car when the weapon was discharged. Tests also revealed traces of gunpowder on her hands that would have resulted from the gun being fired.

Also found in the vehicle was a boxed birthday cake which police say Jane purchased, on the night she died, at a Dartmouth shopping mall and was planning to take to a patient at the rehab centre. Again, investigators speculate Jane purchased the cake in an effort to make them think she had not been planning suicide. Or perhaps she did not decide to kill herself until after she had purchased it. Either way, authorities say, the cake had little bearing on their findings.

In addition to the physical evidence discovered at the scene, the autopsy supports the suicide theory. The examination of the body of Jane Hurshman-Corkum on Monday, February 24, confirmed the presence of a single gunshot wound in the chest. The autopsy revealed the bullet had entered the chest near the centre in the front of the woman's body. In passing through the chest, it caused injury to the right side of the heart and to the lower part of the right lung. Police later recovered the bullet, which passed through her body, in the upholstery of the car seat.

The entry wound indicated the weapon had been in contact with Jane's shirt as it was pressed against her chest. The autopsy also showed Jane had very superficial discolouration of the lower lip, consistent with holding it between the teeth. There were no other injuries found on her body. Authorities said these findings in themselves are consistent with suicide but agreed they do not rule out homicide.

Despite these facts, family members and friends contend Jane was murdered and evidence was planted at the scene of her death in an elaborate plan to make it look like suicide. One vitally important fact, uncovered during the investigation and confirmed by officers with the Halifax Police Department, casts a shadow of doubt upon the suicide theory.

Mysteriously, the driver's side door of the car in which Jane's body was discovered was locked while the other three doors were not. Some insist Jane was shot to death as she was trapped behind the car's steering wheel. Police say there really is no mystery about the locked door as many motorists instinctively lock their door when they fasten their seat belts. Perhaps Jane also had this habit. She may have locked the door to ensure it did not come open after the gun was fired. Or, another theory suggests that Jane locked the door to create a mental barrier for herself before committing suicide. However, those who believe Jane was murdered, believe the door was locked to prevent her from escaping.

These same people also question the location of the gunshot wound as they believe most people who kill themselves with a gun shoot themselves in the head. Authorities rebut this line of thinking by noting statistics suggest most females who kill themselves using a gun do so by shooting themselves in the chest. Furthermore, they argue, Jane was a nursing assistant and as such would have knowledge of the human anatomy, making it conceivable that she would know how to aim the gun to hit a vital organ.

Other evidence found at the death scene can also be discounted according to those who support the concept of a murder plot. For instance, they say it was cold that weekend and any snow that was present on the ground would have been too hard for footprints to show. And the wind was blowing so any fresh footprints in the powdery dusting of snow that fell that weekend in Halifax would have been swept away. They also argue that the car was found in a parking lot where motorists come and go on a regular basis. How many others passed by the vehicle that weekend? How could the police determine which footprints were made that weekend and which were not? Or, in fact, how could they determine if any of the footprints were or were not made by someone either entering or exiting Jane's vehicle?

That there were no strange fingerprints in the car simply suggests that the alleged murderer wore gloves. After all, it was winter. And about the gun powder residue on Jane's hands, opponents of the suicide theory question if police know how long it had been there.

Also of note is the lack of any amount of blood found in the car. Could Jane have been killed someplace else and the car containing her body been left in the parking lot? After all, the vehicle has supposedly been parked for two days in a very busy parking lot, with Jane's dead body inside. Critics of the police investigation say they find it remarkable that no one saw the body for two whole days, yet the parking lot had been used on a steady basis that weekend.

Police say, however, it is customary with the type of gunshot wound that killed Jane there is no substantial loss of blood. As well, they say it is possible that no one saw the body in the car because the vehicle's windows could have been frosted over with condensation.

While all these points can be argued and made to fit either the suicide or murder theory, family members say the fact that there was no suicide note confirms their belief that Jane's death was a homicide. Those who knew Jane say she would not have taken her own life without attempting to explain her motives to her family and friends; they believe she would have placed the well-being of her husband and children ahead of everything else. Had it been suicide, Jane would have left some clue to answer the many questions that now remain in the wake of her death.

Again, police point out, if Jane wanted authorities to think she had been murdered, she would not have left a suicide note. Additionally, they explain, Jane had indicated to many people prior to her death that she had planned to kill herself. In a sense, she had left messages to her family and friends.

Bangs Falls with its one-lane bridge is a small community nestled on the banks of the Medway River. Ultimately, it became the setting for a story of domestic violence so severe that it would shock the nation.

One Foggy Night

Almost ten years earlier, there had been another gunshot. It was a shot that would propel Jane Marie (Stafford) Hurshman into the national limelight.

Greenfield lies about twenty minutes inland from the historic privateering town of Liverpool in Queens County, on Nova Scotia's rugged South Shore. Not far from the centre of Greenfield—in fact only a drive of a few moments along the River Road—is Bangs Falls, a community of less than fifty homes where all the neighbours are like a closely-knit family. A narrow, one-lane bridge extends over the Medway River, where the village straddles both banks.

Until the night of March 11,1982, Bangs Falls had been the home of Jane (Stafford) Hurshman, her common-law husband Billy Stafford, their four-year-old son Darren, and at times, Jane's sixteen-year-old son Allen from a previous marriage. A friend of Billy's, Ronny Wamboldt, also lived at the Stafford home. On that particular night, the serenity of this sleepy Nova Scotian village was shattered by a gunshot, and for some, things have not been the same since.

Like most Maritime spring nights, March 11 was damp and foggy. At around 8:30 p.m. Jane, Billy, and Ronny left their home to go to a friend's party in Charleston, another small Queens County village less than ten miles down the River Road from Greenfield. They stayed there for a few hours and left shortly before 10 p.m.. Although as the designated driver Jane was not permitted to drink, both Billy and Ronny had ingested more than their share of alcohol.

The trio headed back to Bangs Falls using the River Road, a twisting and often treacherous dirt road that follows the Medway River. In the spring this road is often muddy and difficult to drive, especially at night, because of washouts and potholes. Billy sat in the middle of the Jeep's cab next to Jane while Ronny was perched on the passenger side of the truck.

Billy was drunk and as they headed home, he kept telling Jane this was the night that he was finally going to "deal" with their neighbour, Margaret Joudrey, and Jane's son Allen. Margaret was a friend who lived not far from the Stafford house in a trailer. To Jane she was a very close friend and confidant, almost a second mother. In recent weeks Billy and Margaret had begun arguing and tonight he was threatening to burn her trailer. Billy also told Jane he was going to take care of Allen, who had been living with them for a few months.

Jane believed Billy's rantings. She took him seriously because she knew Billy was more than capable of acting upon those threats. Fortunately, by the time the Jeep pulled into the yard of their Bangs Falls home, Billy had passed out in a drunken stupor.

Jane parked the truck about ten feet in front of the small bungalow. On these occasions, Billy had ordered her to remain in the vehicle until he awoke, so she sat quietly waiting for him to come around. It was better to obey his rules than to suffer the violent consequences. Ronny got out of the truck, disappeared inside the house and immediately passed out in bed.

The sound of the truck door closing behind Ronny did not awaken Billy. Jane had no idea how long she might have to sit there, but she knew she could not leave the truck. She sat quietly for about twenty minutes, recalling the threats he had made earlier that evening against Margaret and Allen. Her mind replayed all the ugly scenes; the fear and stifled rage began to surface. As she sat there lost in her memories, she relived the pain she had endured for the past five years in vivid detail. She saw again the painful expressions on the faces of her children every time Billy hit her. She re-experienced the sickness she felt each time Billy hit one of her boys.

Anger and deep resentment overwhelmed her and she decided she could not continue to live under such conditions. She would no longer allow Billy to abuse herself or her children. She made up her mind that she had to act to protect herself and her family. With this determination, she also realized this could be her last chance to escape. She wasn't sure if she had enough courage to do it, but she told herself the time had come; she had to act while the opportunity presented itself. Billy was asleep and now was the time to strike back.

Hoping to summon Allen from inside the house, Jane cautiously blew the truck's horn. She feared the horn might awaken Billy. But it didn't and when Allen failed to come out after a few minutes, she blew the horn again. When Allen appeared in the doorway of the house, Jane instructed him to get a gun from the house and bring it to her.

Not knowing exactly what was happening, Allen went back inside. Billy kept a number of guns around the house and Allen removed a 12-gauge shotgun from Billy's gun rack which hung over the cot where Ronny was now sleeping. He put a shell in the gun, but decided to leave it in the house as he went back outside to double-check with his mother. By this time, Jane was standing outside the truck, near the driver's side door, waiting for her son to return with the gun.

Again she told him to bring her the gun and to be quick about it. This time, Allen did as his mother instructed and brought her the shotgun. With the weapon in hand, she sent him back inside the house where she ordered him to remain.

Timidly, she approached the open window on the driver's side of the truck. Jane wondered if Billy had only been faking to see what she was up to, but there was no movement from inside the vehicle. As Billy slumped inside the cab of the Jeep, Jane gingerly put the shotgun through the open window, rested its barrel in front of his left ear about six inches from his head and pulled the trigger. She didn't look inside the cab after the gunshot. Billy died instantly.

Allen heard the shot inside the house. As he ran outside, he saw his mother standing by the truck. Jane told the boy not to ask any questions. Quickly, she gave him the shotgun, which he instinctively took back inside and laid in the back porch. Then she told him to get her some clean clothes and to put them in a garbage bag. Acting upon her orders, Allen brought her a blouse and a pair of slacks.

By the time he returned, his mother had gotten back into the truck and was sitting behind the steering wheel. Instructing Allen to put the bag on the back of the truck, she told him to take the gun to Margaret's and get rid of it. Jane also told him to phone his grandfather and tell him to meet her by the satellite station in Charleston. Then he was to return to their house and clean up any mess that might be around the yard.

Although covered in blood and body tissue, Jane didn't stop to wash. Her first instinct was to get the truck out of the yard and clean up any trace of what had just happened so that Darren did not see anything when he woke up in the morning. As she pulled out of the driveway she told Allen not to ask any questions, but just to do as she had asked. During the seven-mile drive to Charleston, she never once looked at Billy's body, its upper torso pressing against her as she again navigated the River Road, the same road over which less than an hour ago, she had driven with Billy and Ronny Wamboldt. When she eventually reached her destination in Charleston, she parked the truck on an abandoned road and began walking toward the satellite station where she expected to meet her father.

Meanwhile, back in Bangs Falls, Allen had gone to Margaret's trailer and phoned his grandfather as his mother had demanded. With the help of Roger Manthorne, a man who had been living at Margaret's trailer at the time, he broke the gun down into three pieces and threw it from the one-lane bridge into the Medway River. The river was running fast and deep so they believed it would be a safe place to dispose of the weapon.

Allen then returned to the site where Billy's truck had been parked. Using a rag, he cleaned up blood and body tissue which had splattered over the driveway and the side of the house. He then placed the rag and numerous blood-covered rocks into a plastic bag, took it back to the bridge and threw it into the river. After that was done, he went back to Margaret's trailer to await his mother's return.

By the time Jane reached the satellite station road, her parents, Maurice and Gladys Hurshman, were waiting in their car. Quickly she proceeded to the vehicle and got in the back seat, telling her parents not to ask any questions. She asked them to take her to their place in Danesville, not far from Charleston, where she cleaned up. At her parents' mobile home she bathed and put all the blood-stained clothes in the garbage bag Allen had gotten for her. She then had her parents drive her home. However, because of the condition of the River Road, the Hurshmans chose to take a longer route that would take them along the coast through Brooklyn, Liverpool and Milton.

Eventually, they arrived at the intersection of Bangs Falls road. But instead of taking her all the way to her house, Jane asked her parents to drop her off there. It was several hundred yards to the Stafford house but she gradually made her way home along the muddy roadway, slipping through backyards and wooded areas in an effort to prevent herself from being seen by the neighbours.

It was almost midnight when Jane arrived home. Darren and Ronny were still sleeping and Allen was down at Margaret's trailer. Within minutes, they were reunited. Jane told Allen and her neighbours not to worry because Billy would not be able to bother them again. Allen then burned the garbage bag containing the blood-stained clothes as well as his mother's purse that had been in the truck when Billy was shot.

Jane didn't sleep at all that night, wondering whether Billy was dead. She feared that at any minute he would burst into the house and begin assaulting her. In the morning, mentally and emotionally exhausted from lack of sleep and still unsure if Billy was dead or alive, Jane went to visit Margaret. As she was about to leave her neighbour's trailer, an RCMP police cruiser pulled into the yard.

"Are you Jane Stafford?" the officer inquired.

"Yes," she replied. Police asked if she knew where Billy Stafford was and Jane told them no. She said he had left the previous night and hadn't returned.

When the RCMP officer told her that the body of Billy Stafford had been found earlier that day in his truck, which had been abandoned near Charleston, Jane fainted.

The road sign directs motorists to Bangs Falls in Queens County, a small hamlet near the larger village of Greenfield and about twenty miles from Liverpool. It was Jane Hurshman's road to hell.

The Road to Hell

"I've been to hell, touched it, felt it, and came back again," Jane Hurshman once said about her life with Billy Stafford.

Perhaps on that night Jane had not fully thought about the consequences of her actions but she knew that if it meant going to jail, then so be it. Jail could not be any worse than the life she had been living with Billy Stafford. Jane was no stranger to violence and human suffering. It seemed as if trouble had followed her through her entire life. But nothing could have prepared her for the life she would live with Billy.

Jane Marie Hurshman was born on January 25, 1949, in Brooklyn, Queens County, a small community with its origins closely tied to the newsprint industry and only a short drive from Liverpool. The second of four children born to Maurice and Gladys Hurshman, she was about five years old when she moved with her family from Brooklyn to Truro in May 1954. Maurice was in the army and the family lived there until 1957, when he was transferred to Camp Gagetown in New Brunswick.

The Hurshman family remained in Gagetown for another three years until her father was sent to the Canadian Forces Base in Hemer, West Germany. Although the family moved around a lot during her father's career in the forces, Jane recalled she actually liked the three years she spent in Germany, despite the problems between her parents. "I got to meet a lot of nice people and see many interesting places during those years." They were places that someday she hoped her own children would have the opportunity to visit.

At the end of Maurice's posting in West Germany, the Hurshmans returned to Canada and were relocated to Winnipeg. Her experiences in the harsh Canadian Prairies were not as favorable as those from earlier postings and Jane stayed there with her family for only about six months. At age fifteen, she left the Canadian west and returned to Queens County. It was 1964 when Jane arrived back in Nova Scotia to live with her grandmother.

Jane had many fond memories of her childhood years and of growing up with her older brother Douglas and younger sisters Sandra and Mona, but she also remembered those years as "rough ones," she says. "Dad drank a lot. Most of the time he was drunk; he went to work that way and came home that way." He was always "fighting and hollering," Jane said, recalling that much of his frustration was focused on Jane's mother, Gladys. But she was always quick to point out that although her mother and father fought a lot, Maurice never hit the children.

Her early childhood was filled with sorrow because of the fighting. The years prior to the family's move to Germany were tumultuous ones with Maurice drinking almost constantly and it seemed like he was fighting all the time with her mother. In fact, even though the fighting stopped when the family moved to Germany, the drinking continued. And it continued when the Hurshmans returned to Canada.

"When we came back to Winnipeg, Dad was still drinking and drinking a lot." It was at that point Jane moved back to Nova Scotia. "I wanted to get out of the situation I was in." She believed returning to Queens County would give her the change of pace she was seeking. Upon her arrival back in the Liverpool area, Jane moved in with her grandparents.

Shortly after returning to her hometown Jane met a man, who will be called Murray, while attending a local party one night. He would soon take her on a roller-coaster lifestyle the likes of which she could not even imagine. Two months after her sixteenth birthday, in March 1965, she discovered she was pregnant with the child of this twenty-four-year-old man.

On April 24, 1965, Jane and Murray got married "for all the wrong reasons." The union was not a happy one and after the birth of their son, Allen, later that year on October 9, their relationship continued to deteriorate. "He wasn't violent, but he drank a lot. He lost his work and everything through drinking. The last three or four years I was with him, he didn't work."

The couple lived in Milton, another small Queens County village just north of Liverpool and nestled on the banks of the Mersey River. Despite the hardships, Jane worked to keep the marriage intact. When Allen was seven, a second son, Jamie, was born on October 17, 1972. But life wasn't getting easier and Murray was not working so survival became the first priority.

"He sold a lot of things; he would get money that way." Jane recalled he had no other income except "sometimes he did work on a car for people or something like that and he'd get a few dollars."

Finally, she decided she could no longer live under these conditions. Her youngest child was three when she decided to end the marriage. "I just told him I was going to leave." And she did, although her oldest son Allen wanted to stay with his father to finish school.

It was not easy to make the break from Murray. Jane recalled a day shortly after leaving her husband when she was seeing a lawyer to file for legal separation. She had taken Jamie with her to the appointment. "While I was in seeing the lawyer, they said that I could leave Jamie with the secretary and I did. When I came out, he (her husband) had taken Jamie and was gone."

It was shortly after that incident that Jane began seeing Billy Stafford. He was a friend of her husband's and she believed that seeing another man would make it easier to separate from Murray. By the end of January 1976, Billy and Jane were living together and by the end of May that year, Jane and Murray were divorced.

Although Jane had known Billy casually prior to the breakup of her marriage, she really knew very little about him. She eventually would know more about him than she bargained for.

Lamonte William "Billy" Stafford was born on February 13, 1941, and in 1962 he married a Queens County girl, Pauline Oickle. She was pregnant at the time and over the next six years, the couple had five children. However, after six years, Billy and Pauline split up and she filed for divorce on the grounds of cruelty. Years later, Jane would learn that Pauline had fled to Ontario with her children to escape Billy's madness.

By 1971, Billy had started a new relationship with another Queens County woman, Faith Hatt. Like his previous marriage, this relationship failed and after two years Faith moved to Calgary to get away from Billy Stafford. She was pregnant at the time.

When Jane met Billy, she was on the rebound from a broken

marriage and she had no knowledge of this man's cruel past nor of his reputation for getting into trouble. "I had gone out with him one night and left (my husband) the next night." After the marriage was dissolved, Jane stayed with a friend and Billy visited frequently, bringing her gifts and openly showing his affection. Eventually, she began living with Billy's sister in Bridgewater while he was out on the fishing boats. Finally, they found an apartment in Liverpool and set up their own household.

It was early in 1976, and according to Jane, her relationship with Billy was a good one. She recalls one time that she thought he would be furious with her. "At one point, I had had an accident and I totalled the car coming in from his mother's (in Hunts Point, which is about a ten-minute drive from Liverpool)." Billy was at sea at the time and although Jane had expected him to be angry when he learned of the mishap, "he wasn't upset; he wasn't anything." Instead, "he bought me roses and jewellery. It was good."

In August 1976, Billy and Jane found a home to rent in Charleston, a tiny neighbourhood located near Mill Village on the Medway River famous for its yearly kyack run. They moved there and were very happy at first. It was at that point in their relationship that Jane got pregnant. Darren was born on May 30, 1977, and by the end of August that year, Jane and Billy Stafford had settled in Bangs Falls. Although they never legally married Jane had assumed the name Stafford. However, the relationship was beginning to turn sour.

Thinking back, Jane noted her relationship with Billy Stafford changed after Darren's birth. "Right after Darren was born, Bill started getting different. He said he wanted a baby girl, but we got Darren." Jane had wanted a boy and was pleased when their son was born.

Following the birth of her third son, Jane opted to undergo surgery to prevent further pregnancies. "And he didn't like that idea either." Jane had experienced a great deal of difficulty in the delivery of her second child and doctors had told her she should not have had a third child. Luckily, both Jane and Darren survived the birth, but she felt for the sake of her own health that she should have a hysterectomy.

"I told him that they would operate on me when this one was born." With the operation, however, came an entirely new Billy Stafford. He told her she wasn't any good to him anymore because of the operation. Just about every aspect of her relationship with Billy changed at that

Billy Stafford and Jane Hurshman-Stafford shortly after the birth of their son, Darren, who was born on May 30, 1977.

point. "His speaking; he got violent at different times. He never had a good word for me anymore or anyone else."

Jane didn't leave because she thought the situation would improve. "I just figured things would get better." But they didn't. In fact, the situation grew progressively worse, especially after Billy lost his job on the fishing boats. By November 1977, the physical abuse and beatings had started.

"I don't know if it was just before we moved to Bangs Falls or while we were at Bangs Falls; he had been on a scallop dragger to this point. He had been fishing out of Lunenburg and he had to get off the boat because they blacklisted him and charged him for mutiny." After that Billy only worked sporadically.

"He drew unemployment for that winter (after they moved to Bangs Falls.) I don't know how long he drew that; until he couldn't draw it anymore, I guess." Billy did work the following winter when he got a job with the Canada Works Program to help construct a youth camp at a community not far from where the Staffords lived.

Billy worked very little until 1980 when he found employment on the gypsum boats. This job provided him with sufficient work to allow him to eventually draw unemployment again. "He would work until hunting time and then didn't go to work anymore. He drew unemployment when he got done with the boats."

The pattern continued. In the spring of 1981, he went back on the gypsum boats until September of that year. After the fall of 1981 Bill Stafford was never employed again.

Jane had started working on the first day of September 1977 at Hillsview Acres, a special care facility for the elderly located in Middlefield only a few miles from Bangs Falls. She had been hired as a domestic cleaner, but in less than a month she took a cook's job, a position she maintained for the entire five years she worked at the home. She liked the job, the home, and the people who worked there.

It was around 1980 when Billy started on the gypsum boats that their relationship began worsening and Jane finally realized the circumstances would not improve. "It was bad. I had taken quite a few beatings and the mental abuse…just the hooting and hollering day in and day out, it was a joy to go to work to get away from it all."

The physical abuse started in the spring of 1978, just prior to Darren's first birthday. Actually, she recalled, peculiar things started happening almost immediately after she brought the child home from the hospital, but she had chosen to ignore them. "You couldn't show Darren any love or affection. He didn't have time for him. He didn't pay attention to him at all. He'd just look at him like he was disgusted all the time and call him names. You couldn't get up through the night and feed him like you usually do a baby; he had to sleep all night. He never ever looked after him or done anything for him or with him."

Everything about Jane's own personal relationship with Billy also changed. "There were lots of changes. He told me I wasn't any good anymore; I couldn't have any more kids. He was always putting you down." After the mental abuse started early in 1978, it wasn't long until the physical abuse began.

Jane recalled one incident. "I took Darren to town one time, when he was about six or seven months old; when I had my day off, I always had to take Darren. They were taking pictures in the stores of kids and I took him in and got his picture taken. Bill had been doing something out to the house, putting up cupboards or something, and he had a fellow there helping him. I went in and bought some chicken so that when I came home I didn't have to make supper for them."

She continued, "After I'd gotten home, the other fellow didn't stay that long. After he left, Bill accused me of all kinds of things like the guy paying attention to me and flirting with him and this and that, and he'd just get into a rage and start hitting me. At different times, he'd get into these rages and he didn't know me from Pauline; he would call me Pauline while he was beating me."

The physical abuse was often severe and violent, leaving bruises as proof of the onslaught. Usually, Billy would slap and punch his wife's face. When this happened, he was always under the influence of alcohol and drugs. Despite the pain the abuse caused, Jane did little about the assaults. She became resigned to the way of life she was living.

"If you hear something enough you believe it. When you're told it's your fault or that you're no good, you believe it," she recalled. "I just carried on about my business. He would tell me it was my fault anyway. Whenever I did get a beating, he would always tell me it was my fault; I was the one that started it. You hear it so much that after awhile you begin to believe it is something you do or say."

But she always clung to a thin shred of hope that the beatings would stop. They never did, and as time went on, the beatings and abuse got worse. Jane lost track of the frequency and the times the attacks occurred. Throwing up mental blocks became her only means of self-defence and a way to maintain her sanity in a world that appeared to have gone crazy.

"As the time went on, everything just kept getting worse" and it became difficult to recall the beatings. "You just tried to block everything out and tried to forget about it, hoping it would go away." She knew, though, that Billy's relentless rantings would not stop and it would have been difficult for Jane to recall all of the beatings because on many occasions, they rendered her unconscious.

There was one incident about which Jane could remember the details even if the date was a bit cloudy. She thought it had occurred either in the late fall of 1980 or around February 1981. A friend had been visiting the Stafford household. Up to this point the beatings had happened in the privacy of their home where the secrets were kept well hidden. But on this occasion Billy's guard was down.

Andrea Wamboldt, the wife of Ronny Wamboldt, had been in Toronto for about three years. On this visit back to Queens County she made a point of visiting her friend Jane in Bangs Falls.

"She came out to spend a couple of days with me and we were sitting out in the kitchen. Bill wasn't drinking; he wasn't doing anything. He went in and went to bed. We were sitting there having a few drinks and just talking about old times, not bothering anybody."

The two were taking advantage of the time alone to renew their friendship. The children were sleeping and Billy was in bed.

"We were just sitting there by ourselves. He (Billy) got up and came charging out of the bedroom." He brought with him a loaded .30-.30. "He just pulled the lever down and put it to her (Andrea's) head, grabbed a hold of her and told her to get. It was in the wintertime and was freezing and snowing hard. She didn't have any transportation." But it didn't matter to Billy Stafford that Jane's friend was nearly twenty miles from Liverpool without a vehicle, or that it was late at night in the middle of a winter storm. He had other things on his mind.

"As he was putting her out, he was beating me at the same time. The last thing I remember was that she was gone and he just kept hitting me with the butt of the gun, hitting me in the head. He was telling me that I was a whore and a slut and a tramp. He would say these things over and over."

Jane had no idea what had happened to her friend and no idea what had provoked Billy's rage.

"I knew we had not done anything. He had been in bed; he just came out crazy. His face was blood red and his eyes were right big and bulged out." Billy usually looked like this when he went into his rages. "He would also froth from the mouth like an animal. He didn't have control, it seemed."

At some point in this particular beating, Jane blacked out. "What I remember next is daylight. I was still laying on the kitchen floor and was all wet; I didn't know why I was wet." Jane pulled herself up gradually and made her way to bed. Billy was nowhere to be found. "I don't know where he went when he got up. I didn't know what he did." Jane would later learn that Allen had heard Billy hitting his mother and after the beating had stopped and Billy had gone to bed, he sneaked into the kitchen to see if she was alright. When he found his mother unconscious on the floor, he threw some water on her, hoping to bring her around, and then went back to bed.

This was only one in a long list of beatings that now shook Jane's and Billy's relationship. It was only one of the painful secrets that were kept hidden behind the closed doors of the Stafford household. Physical abuse, torture, mental cruelty, emotional games, and verbal assaults had all become commonplace.

Jane recalled another incident that took place around the Christmas and New Year's holidays of 1981, only a few months before Billy Stafford's reign of terror was brought to an end.

"I don't know if it was right after Christmas or New Year's; but it had been something to do with the holidays anyway." The Staffords were entertaining friends at their Bangs Falls home. There was plenty of alcohol and drugs. "We were all sitting around talking and Bill went to sleep on the chesterfield."

Jane talked with her two guests as Billy slept. "The three of us just sat there and talked and he must have slept for probably an hour or so, maybe a little longer. Then he woke up, or came to, or whatever it was, with that same kind of look. I knew what was coming. He just came over and grabbed hold of me. At that point he was calling me Pauline. He threw me around until I hit the wall and fell down. You'd hit the wall and fall, he'd be right there to grab a hold of you if you did fall down to hit you some more."

The friends stayed all night at the Stafford home and despite their attempts to persuade Billy to stop the rampage, he kept beating her.

"He just turned the stereo on and threw me in the bedroom. They couldn't hear nothing and he just kept hitting me while I was in bed." After that, Jane did not remember anything until the next morning when her friend asked her if she wanted to see a doctor. Billy and the other friend had gone somewhere.

"I don't know why, but I said no." She refused to see a doctor. Jane's face had borne the brunt of Billy's attack. "My eyes were all black and blue; my nose was broken." Her left arm was bruised and her ribs felt like they had been broken. In fact, the beating was so severe that Jane took two weeks off work until the wounds healed.

These were not isolated attacks. "You never knew when they was going to happen." While the physical beatings were often severe, living in fear of his rages was constant psychological abuse.

"Even when you weren't getting beat bad, you'd get slapped around or yelled at and treated like a dog. But even those were better days than the beatings."

Billy Stafford was a tormentor and controller, especially in the family setting, at the dinner table, or while playing cards, one of his favorite pastimes.

"He was always putting everyone down. When we played cards, if you didn't play the right card or do the right thing that he thought you should, he'd hit you—he'd hit me because I was always his partner." And he hit hard — he would often knock Jane right off her chair. It no longer mattered if other people were present to see the violence.

Abuse had become second nature to Billy Stafford and it was not limited to Jane. Her children, especially the young Darren, also knew the fury of his rages.

"From about the time that Darren could walk, Bill never taught him anything good. It was all about how to hate and fight and get ahead of the next fellow the best way he knew how. It didn't matter who he had to hurt."

Along with the emotional torture, Billy introduced his son to guns at an early age. "From about the time he was probably a couple of years old, he always had guns and knives around him. Bill would, at times, just pick him up right by the hair of his head and hold him off the floor and put a butcher knife to his throat. Or he would take him by his feet—his two feet he could hold in one hand—and hold him upside down and take a loaded gun and put it to his head and tell him if he was bad...."

Jane noted that Billy often said this was the way he had raised his other children and Darren would be brought up the same way. "There wasn't hardly any time that Darren wasn't threatened or beaten."

Billy had stunted his son's emotions. "He pretty well held his emotions and feelings inside. When his father was around, he was never allowed to cry because Bill always told him men don't cry. He was told from the time he could walk that he was a man; he wasn't supposed to be a little boy." Further ingraining that belief, Billy would often break or give away the boy's toys, making Darren's childhood a virtual nightmare.

Meal times were the worst.

Billy Stafford with his young son Darren and the family's St. Bernard.

"I would come home from work and make supper. Bill always had Darren sit right alongside of him. Darren was always very nervous. He'd shake and sometimes he'd drop some crumbs off of his spoon or whatever he was using or he'd go to take a drink and he would spill some of his drink. (When this happened) Bill would slap him, knock him down, take whatever was in reach, whether it be a plate, cup, utensils, anything and just hit him over the head, punch him in the face or anything at all. He would have to eat everything, pretty well as much as a grown person. Bill would make him eat it to the point that he would throw it up. Bill would scrape it back in the dish again and feed it to him until it was all gone."

Billy's physical abuse of the child was often extensive and extreme. "One day I was outside. Darren was with me and I was doing something in the flower garden. It was summertime and the windows were open. I had asked Darren to go inside and bring out my cigarettes and he went in to get them." The next thing she knew "I heard Darren crying and Bill hollering. I didn't go in, I just stayed doing what I was doing. He then came over to our bedroom window and stuck a gun out. He fired a shot at me and said 'get in here, old woman, you got a mess to clean up.'"

Jane obediently went inside, fearing that something tragic had happened to her child. "I went in and Bill said 'it's in the bedroom.' He had broken the handle off the mop or the broom, and beat Darren with it. He hit him (so hard) that he messed himself. It was all over the place—the bedroom, the bed…it was a mess."

What she saw when she found Darren in the bedroom, bleeding and trying to choke back his tears, was too much for her. "His body was all black and blue. I started to cry. Darren just laid there; he wasn't allowed to cry. Bill came in when I started to cry and just punched me and told me to get the mess cleaned up, we were going out, and to get the kid dressed, he was going too." After Jane cleaned the bedroom, Darren, and herself, Billy took the family for a drive. "It was the same as if nothing had happened."

After the beatings there was no remorse and no apology. In the year prior to Billy's death, the abuse intensified to the point that he would hit Darren or Jane almost every day.

In addition to the physical and mental abuse, Billy began a routine of perverted sexual abuse that ranged from the bizarre to the sublime, including bestiality and torture. Billy liked to inflict pain as was evident by the frequency of these assaults. For instance, she recalled an incident when he had tied her, naked, to a chair and used a pair of tweezers to pull out her public hair. It was this kind of abuse that left her feeling degraded and dirty. It finally pushed her over the edge.

At this point in the relationship Jane accepted the fact that the abuse had to stop. Other people, including family and friends, knew what was happening in the Stafford household, but no one helped. The police were aware of Billy's violent tendencies and his ability to avoid the law, but still, the authorities seemed powerless to assist Jane and her family. She knew that, someday, someone was going to be killed in their house in Bangs Falls. Jane Hurshman had not only been to hell, but she had lived with the Devil, as Billy Stafford often pointed out to her. She escaped the best way she knew how.

Arrested for Murder

By mid-afternoon of March 12 the word was out that the decapitated body of Billy Stafford had been found in his Jeep near the satellite station road in Charleston. Liverpool RCMP had immediately been called to the scene by local residents who made the gruesome discovery. Upon their investigation, police officers determined Billy Stafford had been shot sometime after 10 p.m. the previous evening. Authorities determined the forty-one-year-old male had been killed by a close-range blast from a shotgun. The possibility of suicide was ruled out— there was no gun at the scene.

Jane's life with Billy Stafford could have ended differently, but she had long ago accepted the fact that the only difference would have been her own death. Those who knew Billy Stafford or who had heard of his reputation expressed different opinions on his death. Many said they knew it would happen "sooner or later" or "he got what he deserved." There were others, however, who expressed sincere sympathy and disbelief that such a "horrible thing" would happen "right here in Queens County."

Even though Jane had found the courage to pull the trigger on the night of March 11, it was not the first time that she had contemplated killing Billy Stafford or taking her own life. On at least two separate occasions, Jane recalled getting out of bed and putting a gun to Billy's head while he was sleeping. However, the thought of Darren seeing the mess had convinced her that Billy could not die in the house. And there were times when the abuse had gotten so extreme that she thought if she couldn't kill Billy then she would kill herself. Reason prevailed though, as she did not want to leave Darren alone with the man who had become his abuser. Jane had also tried to find other people to kill Billy for her. In the end her thinking was anything but rational and she may not have fully thought about the consequences. On March 13, Jane was taken to the Liverpool RCMP detachment for questioning in relation to the shooting. She had told police that Billy had left their home on the night of March 11 and she had no idea where he went or what he had done. However, because of his alleged involvement with drugs, she suggested that maybe the person who had killed Billy Stafford might have been connected to a drug deal.

Jane stuck with this story until finally, exhaustion and emotional strain, coupled with the continuous police questions, led to her confession. She told police everything about the life she and her family had lived with Billy Stafford, about the abuse she and her children had suffered, and about the night of the shooting. In the end, RCMP officers expressed relief that Jane had finally admitted the truth and said she deserved a medal for what she had done. Police actually thought that by killing Billy Stafford, Jane may have inadvertently saved the lives of a number of local officers.

Regardless of any sympathy they may have had toward Jane Hurshman or any contempt they may have held for Billy Stafford, a serious crime had been committed. On March 16, police charged Jane Marie (Stafford) Hurshman with first-degree murder.

A preliminary hearing into the charge was set for early June in the Liverpool courthouse. Jane would be represented by legal aid lawyer Alan Ferrier, who had been working out of Bridgewater. On March 22, she was remanded into custody.

A week later, the story of Jane (Stafford) Hurshman took an unexpected twist when it was confirmed a second individual had been charged with first-degree murder in connection with the death of Billy Stafford. On March 25, police arrested Jane's son, Allen Whynot. In an attempt to cast some doubt around her own guilt, Jane had accused her eldest son of the murder. RCMP reported they made the second arrest once they determined Billy Stafford had been killed in Bangs Falls, and not in Charleston as they had earlier thought. The next day, Jane and Allen were both arraigned on a first-degree murder charge.

In the wake of this new development, Jane was transported to the Halifax Correctional Centre where she had agreed to take a lie-detector test. As a result, the truth was eventually revealed—Jane had been the one who pulled the trigger on the night of March 11. She admitted she had only pointed the finger at Allen because she feared going to jail and leaving Darren behind. Furthermore, she believed the law would go easier on Allen if she said he had shot Billy while she was being beaten.

Within days of her taking the lie-detector test, Jane and Allen were each released on $5000 bail.

Despite the new direction the investigation had taken, the preliminary hearing on June 7,1982, before Judge W.A.D. Gunn of the Provincial Magistrate's Court in Liverpool, determined there was insufficient evidence to bring Allen Whynot to trial in connection with the death of Billy Stafford and his charges were dropped. Jane (Stafford) Hurshman was committed to stand trial at the next setting of the Trial Division of the Nova Scotia Supreme Court in Liverpool.

Although Jane was prepared to enter a guilty plea on a lesser charge of manslaughter, the Nova Scotia Attorney General's Office turned down the plea bargain. Because Billy Stafford was asleep at the time Jane shot him, the Attorney General's Department felt there were sufficient grounds to proceed with a first-degree murder charge.

If Jane was found guilty by the Supreme Court jury of first-degree murder, she would be facing a twenty-five-year prison term without parole. On the night of March 11, was Jane prepared to go to jail for twenty-five years? She later admitted she had not thought that far in advance. All she thought about was getting out from under his control; she saw the opportunity and seized it.

On Trial:
Portrait of a Madman

November 2,1982, was a cold fall morning as the North Atlantic winds nipped at the hordes of people trying to crowd into the court house. Space was limited, and by 9:30 a.m. the courtroom was filled to capacity. Speculation and publicity surrounding Jane's trial had already provided early indications that it was going to be an extraordinary case.

The interior of the courthouse is somewhat plain and simple with one large courtroom and three smaller chambers located in the rear—one for the lawyers on the left side and one for the jury on the right with the middle room being reserved for the presiding judge. The judge's bench stands on an platform under a well-formed arch with desks for the court clerk and recording secretary located directly in front. On both sides of the courtroom are jury stands and situated in the middle is a table for lawyers and other authorities. The witness stand is to the immediate right of the bench.

Although the country's media had not yet picked up the name of Jane Stafford, in a few weeks she would become a nationally-famous figure with her name emblazoned in newspaper headlines and her picture on television screens from coast to coast. By the time the trial concluded, newspaper, radio, and television reporters from across the country would converge on Queens County, all wanting to hear Jane's story. As the trial unfolded, the country would hear the sordid, and at times, unbelievable details of Jane's relationship with Billy Stafford. Initially, it was expected the trial would last two weeks. However, other cases that had been on the docket for this Supreme Court session, including trials for attempted murder, assault, and illegal importation of diamonds, were set over until the next sitting to make way for what was fast becoming a very important case.

The grand jury, after deliberating for about two hours that morning, returned a verdict of "True Bill" in the case of the Crown versus Jane Stafford, meaning the members felt the Crown had shown sufficient evidence to proceed with a trial. The battle had begun.

The afternoon of November 2 saw the selection of the jurors, who along with the judge would form the court for the trial. Approximately one hundred people had been called for jury duty from which twelve were chosen. Initially, ten men and two women were selected, but one woman was later excused by the presiding judge, Supreme Court Justice C.D. Burchell, when it was decided she might not be an impartial juror due to a prior association with the defendant.

That same afternoon, Jane (Stafford) Hurshman, looking tired and worn, stood before the court as she was arraigned on the charge of first-degree murder. Clearly, the months of stress and legal wrangling had

The historic courthouse in downtown Liverpool was the scene of the sensational, headline-grabbing trial of Jane (Stafford) Hurshman, who shot to death her abusive common-law husband in March 1982.

taken their toll. Physically, she hardly looked strong enough to hold a gun, let alone pull the trigger. However, below the surface, Jane was a strong woman. If living under the thumb of Billy Stafford had taught her anything, it was how to persevere in the face of seemingly insurmountable odds. As she stood before the court with lawyer Alan Ferrier at her side, she pleaded not guilty to the charge of first-degree murder.

Days two and three of the trial, November 3 and 4, were held in *voir dire* during which time procedural matters concerning the introduction of evidence were discussed. During these procedures, the court was open to the public, but nothing said in these sessions could be used by the media and the jury was kept out of the courtroom. For anyone who sat through the arguments, those were long days, but they were important as defense and prosecution lawyers debated the use of important pieces of evidence and police statements. For Jane, though, the two days only seemed to prolong the process.

The actual murder trial began on Friday, November 5, with the Crown presenting its case. Over the course of the trial, the Crown anticipated that about sixty witnesses could be called; of those, some thirty would be for the prosecution.

As the trial began, Jane assumed her assigned station in front of the bench. Seated next to her lawyer with her head bowed and her eyes downcast, her slender body often slumped from fatigue. It was almost as if she was trying to muster enough strength from within herself to remain seated in the hardwood chair that was designated for the accused. Over the next two weeks, this would become a familiar position for Jane.

Blaine Allaby, Crown Prosecutor, appeared confident as he addressed the jury. His ultimate goal was to present sufficient evidence to show the jury that Jane had committed premeditated murder and in his opening address he said he would prove she did "willfully and unlawfully plan the death of Billy Stafford." Following his brief but pointed introduction, Allaby began calling his processional of witnesses to the stand. In particular, he called individuals who had prior associations with Jane, including people with whom she had worked at Hillsview Acres, a life insurance agent who confirmed Jane had taken out a policy on Billy, and a man who testified the accused had approached him with a proposition to have Billy killed.

The testimony of Beverly Taylor, a fisherman from Riverport in Lunenburg County, was an important piece of evidence in the Crown's case because it was considered to be proof that Jane had planned Billy's death for some time. And the existence of the insurance policy, which it was said Billy knew nothing of, provided further collaboration for that plan. Taking the witness stand, Beverly Taylor confirmed he had known Billy Stafford for a number of years through their association on the local fishing boats. Taylor acknowledged that he had met Jane on a number of occasions during the months prior to Billy's death. Under oath, he admitted that Jane had asked him if he would shoot Billy for a sum of $20,000. Or, she had asked that if he wouldn't do it himself, maybe he could help her find someone else who would.

In his testimony, Beverly Taylor pointed out that during these dealings with the accused, she appeared to be "desperate" and he said she "looked like a woman under great strain." However, he told the court he would not go for Jane's plan because he felt Billy might, in some way, have been behind the scheme.

Collaborating testimony by other witnesses confirmed that Jane Stafford had, in May 1981, taken out an insurance policy valued at $20,000 on the entire family and that it appeared Billy did not know the policy existed as Jane had signed his name and the papers were kept at a neighbour's house. However, defense lawyer Alan Ferrier, in cross-examining, pointed out the policy covered the entire family, not just the husband. Furthermore, he noted, under certain circumstances, such as when the husband is on a fishing boat, it is common practice for the wife to sign her husband's name.

Later the same day, the Crown called another witness, Ronald "Ronny" Wamboldt, to the stand. It was his testimony that would introduce the jury to the barbaric Billy Stafford. Wamboldt had been living with the Staffords prior to and at the time of the incident and was known to be an alcoholic who considered himself Billy Stafford's friend. Wamboldt recounted stories of abuse that members of the Stafford household, including himself, were alleged to have suffered at the hands of Billy Stafford. Not a day would go by in which Billy wasn't fighting with Jane, he confirmed, pointing out that Billy would "push her at least two or three times a day."

A man of frail stature, he became somewhat intimidated by the whole court structure and blurted out the whole story. Wamboldt spoke of the deceased man's house rules and of how when they sat down at the table to eat, "Everyone had to follow Billy's pace. If they didn't follow

Billy's example, they would receive a beating from him." He related the incident in which the Staffords' four-year-old son, Darren, was not eating as fast as his father. He confirmed he saw Billy force food down the child's throat, causing the boy to vomit. "He just scraped it up in his plate and made him eat it again."

Billy was described by Wamboldt as a controller, a man who liked to see others suffer, and admitted that on numerous occasions he had seen Billy fire a gun at people. And, he added, Billy often pointed guns at him as well to further intimidate him.

In fact, Wamboldt's testimony confirmed that Billy's control of the people who resided in the little bungalow in Bangs Falls was so extreme that "he hit us for no good reason." Many times, he said, he had witnessed Billy "hit the children or beat up" Jane even when he appeared to be in good spirits. When Billy was in a good mood, it didn't mean that he wouldn't hit anyone. He had often seen Billy's mood change in just a matter of seconds.

Unbelievably, the people who lived in the Stafford house didn't complain about the way Billy treated them because, Wamboldt said, "we knew better. He'd give you another smash" if you did. Continuing to paint the picture of an evil man under Ferrier's questioning, the witness elaborated on Billy's attitude toward God and the Bible. "He said he was sent by the Devil." For example, although Billy was born on Thursday, February 13, 1941, he told people his birthday was on a Friday. Being born on a Friday the 13th gave substance to his claims that the Devil had sent him and it was symbolic of the evil person he actually was. Wamboldt told the court that at no time would Billy allow a Bible in his house, nor would he allow any talk about God. "But he talked about the Devil a lot."

The truth about Billy Stafford was coming out through the testimony of the witnesses who were called to the stand. To people who had been sheltered all their lives from the horrors and tragedy of domestic violence, the evidence was difficult to digest. However, the worst was yet to come.

The afternoon of that same day saw another Crown witness take the stand. Allen Whynot, Jane's sixteen-year-old son, told his story of the night Billy Stafford died.

Darren, his younger brother, was asleep and he was watching television, he recalled with some authority. Despite his age, Allen would prove to be a credible witness not only for the Crown but for the defence as well. Shortly after he heard the truck pull into the driveway and heard Ronny Wamboldt come into the house, his mother had summoned him outside by blowing the horn. He admitted that his mother then instructed him to get a gun, which he did, and he testified that at this point Billy appeared to be sleeping. After returning to the house, he said he "heard a gunshot" and then went back out to the truck.

There he found his mother standing by the truck with the gun in her hands. He told the court of the events that then unfolded; of how his mother had instructed him to "go down to Margaret Joudrey's, get rid of the gun, and to get her some clean clothes." Finally, he admitted he had called his grandfather, Maurice Hurshman, and told him to meet his mother at the satellite station, as she had requested.

According to his testimony, while Jane was gone, he and Roger Manthorne broke the gun down into three pieces and then disposed of it by standing on the Bangs Falls bridge and throwing them into the Medway River. He then told of returning to the house where he wiped blood spots off the house with a cloth, picked up some blood-covered stones, placed them in a bag and threw them into the river as well.

He recalled that when his mother returned later that night, she had on the clean clothes he had gotten her and she was washed up. He told how he then took the clothes she had been wearing at the time of the shooting, along with her purse, and burned them in the stove in an attempt to get rid of the evidence.

Allen also testified to the abuse he and others had suffered from Billy Stafford and he confirmed earlier testimony of abuse and torture in the Stafford household when he told of how Billy would beat his younger brother, Darren, "with his fist, a stick or plate. Whatever he had in his hands." Allen also admitted that he, too, would be beaten by Billy at least once a week "for no reason."

Allen vividly related an incident which occurred one morning when his mother was putting wood in the stove "and Billy fired a .22 at her." He also remembered another time when Jane was working in the garden and Billy shot at her from inside the house through an open window.

Generally, the young witness continued, Billy treated his mother badly every day. He told of countless incidents when he found his mother unconscious on the floor after being beaten by Billy and how he had seen Billy hit his mother with a vacuum cleaner hose or how he would often fire a gun at her. Allen remembered a conversation he once had with his mother after he had told her she didn't look good. It was then, he said, that Jane had told her son she couldn't "live like this" anymore.

The teenage boy who had taken his mother the gun on the night of March 11, 1982, described Billy as a controller and a man on the edge. Billy had complete control over the house because "everyone was afraid of him." No one, he continued, could leave the house because they were afraid Billy would follow them. On one occasion he had heard his mother tell Billy she was leaving and Billy responded by telling her that if she left he would kill her mother, father, sisters, and then he would find and kill her.

Allen described the situation at the Stafford household prior to Billy's death as getting progressively worse every day, and according to his testimony, even the animals were abused by Billy. "They were afraid of him too," he said. For instance, the St. Bernard that Billy had kept had been driven crazy because of the constant beatings it received. On a regular basis, "Billy would kick the dog in the mouth, bite its nose, and hit it with a piece of wood for no reason."

The testimony of Ronny Wamboldt and Allen Whynot confirmed the Stafford home had been a house of horrors under the control of an abusive and sadistic madman. By now the community was abuzz with talk of the trial and it seemed no matter where one went, the topic of discussion was Jane and Billy Stafford. Despite the testimony that was coming out through the trial, many local residents still couldn't believe the stories. Instead, they chose to believe that the tales of abuse were an elaborate defense plan to "get her off."

Because of other trials that had taken place at the Liverpool courthouse prior to these proceedings, the Queens County justice system had developed a reputation for being lenient on even those who committed the most serious of crimes, including murder. The popular saying around the community was, "If you want to kill somebody and get away with it, do it in Queens County."

Even some of the most die-hard sceptics eventually came to believe the stories that were being told about Billy Stafford, but there were others who were adamant in their disbelief and resented the fact that, in their opinion, Billy Stafford was being put on trial and not Jane Stafford. Despite this line of thinking which, at this time, was held by a minority, the trial of Jane Stafford had begun to pick up steam and attract national attention. That in itself made some local residents resent Jane Stafford because they felt she was attracting negative publicity to their community.

By and large, though, the groundswell of support for Jane was growing. Her trial attracted many curious onlookers, some of whom wanted to hear the morbid testimony first-hand while others wanted to get a glimpse for themselves of this local woman who was becoming so famous. Additionally, there were others who were there to give her support because the trial was breaking new ground, and regardless of who liked or disliked it, the fact remained that this woman was becoming a hero in the fight against domestic violence and wife abuse.

Following a weekend recess, the murder trial resumed on Monday, November 8, with the Crown continuing its presentation in an attempt to prove that Jane did indeed, commit first-degree murder. By this time, she had withdrawn into the safety of her own world, allowing only close contact with her family. Coming to court each day proved to be a challenge as the media crush began. Jane's physical strength was slipping away as was evident by the fit of her now-baggy clothes. With her face showing signs of constant worry, she became a picture of a desperate woman; a person struggling to cope with the world around her, a world that was spinning out of control.

Crown witness Roger Manthorne, the neighbour who lived at Margaret Joudrey's trailer, testified that after knowing Billy Stafford for quite a long time, he himself had very little trouble with the man. Manthorne testified to his involvement in the events which unfolded on the night of March 11. He recalled that he and Margaret Joudrey were at home that evening.

"Allen came down at around 9:30 or so that night," he thought. "He came in and laid a gun in the porch and asked if he could use the phone." Upon receiving permission, Manthorne saw the boy make a phone call, but he didn't know to whom. He then admitted that he went along when Allen asked him if he would help dispose of the gun. However, he vehemently pointed out, he refused to go back to the bridge the second time when the boy wanted to get rid of the plastic bag which contained the blood-stained rags and rocks.

Again trying to illustrate that Jane had been planning to kill Billy for some time, Allaby asked Manthorne to speak about the occasion when she had asked him for some pills. The witness testified he had a heart condition for which he was taking medication. He remembered one occasion when Jane had sent down to the trailer for some pills, but he pointed out he had no idea what she wanted with them. As far as he could remember, this had happened "about a month" before the shooting.

In the cross-examination by Ferrier, the witness revealed he was surprised at the events which took place on the night in question. Although he confirmed that he had suspected "something was happening" in the Stafford house, "I never thought she would have enough gumption to kill someone."

During his testimony, Manthorne referred to many arguments Billy and Margaret Joudrey had with each other over "who owned what" piece of property. He reported that in the two-and-a-half years he had lived there, the pair had quite a number of arguments over land boundaries. He also related an incident in which a bullet was discovered just outside their house and confirmed that Margaret Joudrey also kept guns in the house, including one which hung directly over the bed.

Following Manthorne's testimony, Margaret Joudrey was called to the stand. Appearing reluctant to take the stand, she was on the defensive from the very minute she took the oath. She agreed she had treated Jane like her own daughter and that they had always gotten along quite well until the night of March 11. But since that night, she stressed, their relationship had been almost severed and she blamed Jane for getting her into so much trouble that she had to come to court.

Always quick with a rebuttal, Joudrey attempted to discredit testimony from earlier witnesses about arguments she supposedly had with Billy Stafford and about abuse that Jane had allegedly suffered. She emphasized that she had never personally seen anything. Aptly described as an hostile witness, Joudrey said she was not surprised when she heard about the shooting because "I figured it had been planned for quite some time."

According to Joudrey, Jane had often made "secret" phone calls from her trailer and confirmed that she would often tend house while Jane went to meetings with people. Joudrey also confirmed that Jane had kept the insurance policy, about which she stated Billy apparently knew nothing, at her house so he would not find it.

Further into her testimony, under the insistent questioning of Ferrier, Joudrey denied being afraid of Billy Stafford. She also denied keeping loaded guns in her house and she stated that when Jane tried to confide in her about what was happening with Billy, she ignored her. "She complained a lot but I didn't pay any attention to her because she told so many lies." The woman who claimed she had taken Jane to be her daughter denied ever having taken care of Jane on occasions when she was ill in bed following a beating. "I never saw any bruises and I never saw Billy hit her."

Although avoiding eye contact with the witness, Jane shook her head in disbelief at what she was hearing. Could this be the same woman she had trusted and loved? She sat expressionless as Joudrey continued.

Despite Joudrey's attempts to avoid giving specific details about her relationship with Billy and Jane, Ferrier persisted and at times Justice Burchell had to order the witness to answer the lawyer's questions. Finally, Joudrey did admit that Jane had kept a Bible at her trailer because Billy would not allow it in their own home. She also agreed that Billy did get "a little weird" at times, but quickly clarified her statement by pointing out that "everyone gets a little weird sometimes."

Ultimately, however, Joudrey continued to insist she was not afraid of Billy Stafford and continued to deny that she had witnessed any abuse. Jane slouched in her chair; she could not believe what she was hearing.

As the trial continued that Monday, the jury heard from witnesses who had discovered the truck and body of Billy Stafford near Charleston. That afternoon, exhibits such as blood-stained gravel were introduced into evidence. Wrapping up the proceedings of November 8, Jane's parents, Morris and Gladys Hurshman, took the stand, testifying to the events of the night of March 11 when they were contacted by Allen. Her parents confirmed they had received a phone call from their grandson and shortly thereafter went to the satellite station road where they picked up Jane. From there, the trio returned to their home where Jane showered. They then drove their daughter back to her Bangs Falls home.

Nodding from across the courtroom almost as if to give her consent, Jane listened intently as her parents spoke. "Jane never told us anything and we never asked any questions," they claimed.

In total, Crown Prosecutor Blaine Allaby called 31 witnesses in an attempt to prove that Jane, in taking the life of her common-law husband Billy Stafford, had committed first-degree murder. Included among the witnesses were members of the Royal Canadian Mounted Police. In fact, RCMP testimony dominated most of the trial on Tuesday, November 9.

As expert testimony was being entered into evidence, pictures of the truck and the decapitated body of Billy Stafford were circulated to the jury. Explaining the graphic pictures, Corporal Philip Campbell, a forensic firearms expert from Halifax, testified that from the evidence presented to him, he would estimate the deceased had been shot from a range of six inches or less, "to cause such gross destruction of the victim's skull." Illustrating with his hands, he explained when a shotgun is fired at such close range, "it literally causes the skull to explode." If the weapon had not been held as close, the skull would not have exploded because the gases emitted when it was fired would have been able to vent to the sides of the muzzle. But he said, "When the barrel is held within six inches of the skull, the gases enter the head, causing an explosion." From skin samples he had examined, Corp. Campbell said all evidence indicated the gun that killed Billy Stafford "had been held at an extremely close range."

Following Corp. Campbell's testimony, the Crown called serology and toxicology experts who testified concerning blood and body fluid samples from the victim. As well, the expert witnesses testified concerning drug content in the victim's body and they confirmed no common prescription drugs could be traced in the victim's blood.

Corporal Vic Gorman of the Yarmouth RCMP detachment, one of the many officers called to the scene, testified the truck had been full of blood and brain particles, "as though an explosion had taken place inside."

During the afternoon proceedings, a pathologist's report was entered into evidence. The report confirmed the deceased had died from a gunshot wound to the head. It further stated the projectile had entered the skull in front of the left ear and exited near the right ear. The report also supported the theory that the gun had been held within six inches of the head.

A number of other Crown witnesses were called, mostly RCMP officers involved in the investigation. One of those officers was Constable Susan Ivany from the Bridgewater detachment. She testified that she had accompanied Jane to the Liverpool station on March 14. She told of a bruise which had been discovered on Jane's left arm which was estimated to have been approximately three-and-a-half inches in length and one inch wide. In cross-examining, Alan Ferrier asked about photographs which had been taken of the bruise. Constable Ivany replied she had never seen them, but had been told they did not turn out. As well, she acknowledged no photographs of the bruise were entered as evidence.

Media reports later inferred the bruise may have been the result of a gun recoiling.

Testimony on November 10 centred upon two statements given by the accused. Staff Sergeant Peter Williamson of the Liverpool RCMP detachment testified that on March 25 he had taken a statement from Jane Stafford. He described her condition that day as "cool, calm and collected." He noted she did not seem excited and he felt he could talk with her casually.

Best defined as a no-nonsence police officer, Staff Sergeant Williamson read the statement that he had taken. It said Allen had shot Billy. In the statement, Jane said when they (Billy, Ronny Wamboldt, and herself) had gotten home that night, "Billy had been drunk and told Ronny to 'get the fuck out.' He then said that night was the night he was going to 'get even' with Margaret." He told Jane he had gotten a can of gas and was going to throw it onto the Joudrey trailer. And then he was going to deal with Allen.

In the statement referred to by Staff Sergeant Williamson, Jane said she had told Billy that he couldn't do those things. "He then started hitting her on the head." The statement said Jane's head fell on the steering wheel and the horn started blowing.

Jane reportedly said it was then that she heard the noise of a gunshot and saw something in white go past the front of the truck as she looked up. "She figured it was Allen because he had been home; she had recognized the white shirt as his."

Everyone makes mistakes under stress and Jane later admitted that accusing her son of killing Billy Stafford was wrong. It may have been grasping at straws, but initially, Jane believed the law would go easier on the boy if police believed he was protecting his mother. Trying to implicate Allen in Billy's death was something Jane regretted and she knew there was no explanation for her actions. However, she hoped her son would someday forgive her for what she had done.

In the cross-examination, Staff Sergeant Williamson confirmed he had found Billy Stafford, from his own personal dealings with him, to be a violent man. And, he pointed out, he had warned his officers that if they ever received a call about Billy Stafford, "they should go armed." Williamson also testified that police knew Billy had been connected with drugs and deer jackings on an ongoing basis. With reference to Billy's driving, the RCMP officer explained an average person could be expected to have three or four entries on their record over a period of twenty years, but Billy's stats had filled three or four cards.

The staff sergeant also admitted that following Billy's death he had said to other police officers, but not directly to Jane, "that she deserved a medal for what she had done." He felt she had probably saved the lives of a couple of police officers who had been threatened by Billy. Such testimony from a police officer shocked the courtroom.

RCMP Corporal Howard "Howie" Pike, the final Crown witness, testified that after Jane had taken a lie-detector test, he had taken a second statement from Jane on March 27 at which time she confessed and said, "I killed him…in the truck in our yard. Ronny went in the house. Bill was drunk, passed out. I waited for about twenty minutes, then I blew the horn. Allen came out of the house and I told him to get me a gun. I got out of the truck and Allen brought me the gun. I laid the gun on the window of the driver's side. I pulled the trigger. It was a mess of blood and stuff. I told Allen to go to Margaret's to phone Nan and tell them, Margaret and Roger, it was all right, he wouldn't hurt Margaret anymore."

Corp. Pike noted that after she gave this second statement, Jane appeared to be more relaxed and "said she was sorry for what had happened; she was sorry for the trouble she had caused, and she said she was glad it was over."

With the Crown concluding its case, the trial was recessed until November 16.

The Defence Rests

When the trial resumed on November 16, the eyes of the nation were beginning to focus on the little historic courtroom in Liverpool, N.S. When proceedings got underway, Jane listened intently as defence counsellor Alan Ferrier opened his address to the jury. Her heart beat faster and her breathing seemed tight as she heard her lawyer begin the counter-offensive. She knew her fate and her future rested in his hands. Ferrier began by pointing out that the evidence presented by the Crown raised a number of questions and problems concerning the first-degree murder charge.

Ferrier's theory was that Jane Stafford had acted in the heat of passion on the night of March 11. He reasoned that Jane had shot Billy Stafford as an impulsive reaction to what he had said about taking care of Allen and Margaret. There was no premeditation that night. In fact, he stressed, "she didn't think at all about her actions." In an attempt to prove Jane's innocence of the first-degree murder charge, Ferrier called a total of 16 witnesses, including the defendant's mother and the defendant herself along with Billy's first common-law wife and his former legal wife.

Trying to illustrate how Jane's behaviour was a learned response, Ferrier called her mother, Gladys Hurshman, who testified that she had suffered similar treatment from Jane's father and that her children had seen this on many occasions.

Following her mother's testimony, Jane took the stand. For more than four hours, the defendant revealed the most intimate and painful details of her life to the spectator-packed courtroom, relating her early childhood, her first marriage and her life with Billy Stafford. She described her first husband as an alcoholic, saying, "He wasn't a violent man, but he drank a lot and had lost his job through drinking."

A tall, thin woman, Jane appeared very nervous as she began to relate her experiences with Billy Stafford. She spoke in a barely audible monotone, almost void of any emotion. But she appeared steady as she began her testimony. Jane explained that after leaving her first husband, she went to live with Billy and at the beginning they had gotten along well.

However, she continued, when their son Darren was born, "things started getting different. He wanted a baby girl" and she said he did not like the idea that Jane had agreed to surgery to prevent herself from getting pregnant again. "Just about everything changed. He was violent all the time and never spoke good of anyone." And, she explained, she didn't leave because "I thought things would get better."

The defendant told of numerous instances of abuse and torture she had suffered at the hands of Billy Stafford, pointing out that near the end, "It was a joy to go to work just to get rid of him."

Although the jury had heard many horrendous tales about Billy's rantings and illegal behaviour, nothing could have prepared them for the testimony that Jane was about to give. Nothing, not even in their wildest imaginations, could have prepared the eleven members of the jury for the litany of horrors they were about to hear. Publicly, citizens expressed shock and utter disbelief at the stories of abuse that this man had supposedly committed against his common-law wife and his own child. Through her testimony as well as that of other witnesses who had taken the stand prior to her appearance and those who were yet to follow, the defence painted a vivid portrait of a wife batterer and child abuser.

For what seemed like an eternity, Jane recounted her life with Billy Stafford. For more than four hours, Jane kept the court riveted as she took members of the jury and all those present on an emotional rollercoaster ride. While acknowledging that in her mind Billy had her trapped, Jane described him as "like an animal" when he got into these rages, saying his face would get red, his eyes would bulge out and "he would froth at the mouth." She told of incident after incident in which she suffered unspeakable acts of abuse at the hands of Billy Stafford and she explained that she never knew when the attacks would happen, "not that you could ever be prepared for them, even if you did know. Even when you weren't getting beaten badly, you always would be getting slapped around and being used worse than a dog." These mild forms of assault and verbal taunts occurred on "the better days," she added.

If the stories of physical and emotional abuse were shocking, nothing prepared the jury for the tales of the sexual abuse Jane had forced on her. She described numerous unusual experiences in her relationship with Billy. Addressing an outwardly disgusted jury, she related a bizarre, perverted sexual life, complete with bondage, torture, sodomy, and beastiality. But she quickly pointed out that before Darren was born their sexual life had been normal. However, from the time their child was born, Billy began to make strange demands and practiced sadistic and perverted sexual acts. She knew the jury must have been disgusted by these facts and she felt dirty for repeating them; but, after all, it was the truth and the court had to know everything.

There were many times that Billy had forced her to perform unnatural sexual acts and while the physical beatings were painful, this abuse made her feel inhuman. Recounting the litany of horrors, Jane told the court of the unusual rituals Billy often performed, including anal intercourse. When this happened, she said, the pain was dreadful, like she was being torn apart. Billy must have also found it uncomfortable as well because on one occasion he smeared a piece of solid plastic plumbing pipe, about one inch in diameter and four or five inches in length, with Vaseline and forced it into Jane's rectum. She was forbidden to remove the pipe whenever Billy was home unless she was going to work or unless he wanted to have sex.

This sadistic routine continued for months, and while it was one of the most painful forms of torture, it was only one of many to which she was subjected by her abusive mate.

Feeling humiliated and used, Jane said that on many occasions she protested, but was made to suffer unimaginable consequences as Billy seemed to derive some sort of pleasure at making her suffer. When asked by the prosecution why she hadn't gone for help, she replied, "I knew it would be no good; it seemed he got away with everything."

Jane said she had grown to hate Bill Stafford by this time. "I wanted him dead and there was no way of leaving him in my mind." She believed the threats that he had made about killing her family if she ever tried to leave. She admitted that in January of 1982, she had approached Beverly Taylor and said matter-of-factly without any apparent remorse, "I asked him if he would kill Bill."

During that day in the court proceedings, Jane also related the incidents of March 11, recalling that Billy "kept raving about how he was going to get Margaret that night and how he was going to deal with Allen." She testified that Billy said, "We may as well clear everything up in one night."

Jane openly and willingly admitted to shooting Billy Stafford that night. She explained to the members of the jury that during the drive home Billy had passed out; that when they arrived home, Ronny Wamboldt got out and went into the house. "I stayed in the truck; whenever he passed out in the truck, I'd have to stay until he woke up. I just sat there; everything he had said about what he was going to do started sinking in; I finally said to hell with it, I wasn't going to live like that anymore...I put the gun in the window and pulled the trigger."

Further along in her testimony, Jane admitted that, in fact, on two prior occasions after being beaten, she had taken a gun and put it to Billy's head while he was sleeping, "but I couldn't do it." She didn't want Darren to see anything. She also said that, contrary to what other witnesses had said, Billy had known the insurance policy existed.

In his re-examination, Ferrier asked why she had taken Billy's threats to kill her and her family so seriously. Jane replied without hesitation, "I knew he would do it because he had done it before." She then told the story of how Billy had often bragged to her about killing a fellow fisherman when they were on a trip and that he had gotten away with it. Indeed, it is a fact that Billy Stafford was on the same boat on February 14, 1974, from which a young Liverpool man, Jimmy LeBlanc, went missing. Although his death was never investigated, unofficially authorities said LeBlanc accidentally fell overboard and was lost at sea. It was thought that Billy did not make idle threats and even today, more than a decade after his death, none of the crew members who were on board the boat that day will talk about what happened to young LeBlanc.

Jane assured the jury that even if police said Jimmy LeBlanc had fallen overboard, Billy said otherwise and he often related his version of the events of February 14, 1974. "'Jimmy didn't go over by his own steam,' he would say. He told me he killed before and he would go it again," Jane claimed. Considering the circumstances of LeBlanc's mysterious death and the realities of her own existence, Jane feared that if Billy could kill once and get away with it, "he could do it again."

Jane stepped down from the witness stand exhausted and emotionally drained. Yet she didn't feel any regrets. Instead, she felt relieved, as if an enormous weight had been lifted off her shoulders.

Dr. Rose Marie Sampson, a psychologist, and Dr. Caroline Abbott, a psychiatrist, also testified that day and both agreed that Jane had acted under enormous stress on March 11. Both doctors felt Jane was incapable of planning ahead, that the actions which immediately followed the shooting were merely incidental, and that she had responded out of confusion and shock.

Dr. John Dimock, a forensic and child psychiatrist from the Royal Ottawa Hospital, also testified concerning the mental well-being of Darren. The doctor reported the youngster "had been exposed to severe emotional abuse. I would see him as being a child who would need a lot of help."

He noted when he had asked Darren what three wishes he would want granted, "He replied he would like some toys; some paper and pens; and he wished he was as big as his father, that his father was small and that he could be mean to him." He said this type of response is common in children who are often abused.

Dr. Dimock also testified to interviewing Jane Stafford during some of his sessions with Darren. Based on his extensive work on domestic violence and wife abuse, he was not at all surprised that Jane was not aware that help could have been found through a transition house or some other type of agency. It is common for abused women to feel isolated, alone, and cut off from the rest of the world.

"There's a lot of shame and a lot of fear," he pointed out, noting that abused women often blame themselves for what is happening in the relationship. This is especially true in women who come from an abusive home environment where they may have seen their father batter and assault their mother. Under these circumstances, Dr. Dimock added, the pattern continues because abused women come to believe that this is normal behaviour in a marriage.

Responding to questions from Crown Prosecutor Allaby, Dr. Dimock said he believed Jane removed the body of Billy Stafford because she did not want her young child, Darren, to see anything. First and foremost in her thinking was the safety and well-being of her children and he suggested Jane would go to any lengths to protect and shelter them.

The string of witnesses which followed the doctor continued for the rest of the day and continued until November 18. Witness after witness related their own stories of Billy's abuse. The fourteenth defence witness was Billy's first common-law wife, Faith Hatt. "It was pretty good in the beginning, but it got so bad at the end that I had to leave because I couldn't take it anymore." The court heard that Faith, pregnant with Billy's child, fled to Calgary to escape his clutches.

It was Billy's former legal wife, Pauline (Oickle) Stafford, who gave credence to Jane's story because her tale was so painfully similar. "He was a very cruel man during the six years that I was married to him." Pauline told of incidents when Billy had hit her and kicked her while she was pregnant. Once, she said, "he almost drowned me in a bucket of water."

Pauline and Billy had five children and she confirmed he would often beat them quite badly from the time they were about six months old. She testified about the time that Billy had hit their eldest daughter with a wooden chair rocker. He would stand another child outside the house and throw knives at her to see how close he could come. And he would sit the children on the steps with lit cigarettes and make them eat the butts. "The children were terrified of him," she stressed.

Both of Billy's former wives admitted they had been frightened of him and said they knew they would not be able to stay in Queens County once they broke up with him. So Faith went to Alberta and did not return until three years before Billy's death. Pauline moved to Ontario where she was still residing at the time of the trial.

After calling another witness to confirm Pauline's story the defence rested.

During the afternoon of November 18, the jury heard closing statements from both the Crown and defence, at which time Prosecutor Allaby said, "This is an important case to all those battered women in society."

Ferrier, on the other hand, asked the jury to consider beyond a reasonable doubt if the Crown had shown Jane (Stafford) Hurshman had deliberately planned the death of her common-law husband on the night of March 11, 1982. Why, on this night, would she kill the man when he was sleeping in the truck when on other occasions she could have killed him following a beating while she had bruises to prove the horror stories? He suggested Jane had acted in the heat of the moment, when the opportunity to get away from Billy Stafford had presented itself, and he urged the jury to find Jane guilty not of first-degree murder but to return a verdict of manslaughter.

On the following day, November 19, the jury was charged by Supreme Court Justice C.D. Burchell in an address that lasted seven and a half hours. For the first two hours, he instructed the jury on the law connected with the first-degree murder charge. He told the jury it could return one of four verdicts, but if a guilty verdict was returned, the jurors must be sure, beyond a reasonable doubt, that the accused had willfully and deliberately committed the crime.

The jury had four choices—guilty of first-degree murder, guilty of second-degree murder, guilty of manslaughter or not guilty, which seemed out of the question to Jane. Justice Burchell explained in detail how each verdict could be reached. After informing the jury of the law, he then went on to review the testimony of each of the forty-six witnesses, saying he felt it was necessary because of the length of the trial.

The jury deliberated from 5:30 on Friday evening, November 19, and returned a verdict at approximately 11:30 the next morning. After being sequestered for eighteen hours, the eleven-member jury returned a "not guilty" verdict in the Crown versus Jane (Stafford) Hurshman.

Following that announcement, spectators in the courtroom burst into tears, and rounds of applause came from those who were obviously pleased with the jury's decision. Many people outwardly showed their gratitude for the verdict and some thanked a higher power as a number of onlookers openly exclaimed, "Praise the Lord."

It was an emotion-packed couple of minutes for Jane (Stafford) Hurshman who "never in my wildest dreams" thought the jury would find her not guilty. As she stood before the judge, holding the hand of her lawyer, Jane seemed somewhat stunned by the verdict. She and Ferrier remained motionless until the excitement in the courtroom subsided. Jane's family, who had remained loyal to her throughout the trial, appeared relieved as they sat, wiping the tears from their eyes, obviously overwhelmed by emotion.

Instinctively, reporters in the courtroom pushed toward the woman who had just been found not guilty of murder after publicly admitting she had killed her common-law husband. Commenting on the jury's declaration, Jane replied it felt "super to have the ordeal over with" and "I thank God for their decision."

However, the jubilation would be short-lived. Almost immediately—that same morning following the verdict—the Crown began making suggestions that it would appeal the jury's decision. Allaby left the courtroom without making a comment.

*Jane (Stafford) Hurshman with her defence lawyer Alan Ferrier on
the steps of the Liverpool courthouse on Saturday morning,
November 20, 1982, the day the jury returned with a not-guilty
verdict.*

For the immediate future, though, there was reason to celebrate. As the crowds in front of the now-famous Liverpool courthouse slowly dwindled, Jane made her way out of the building to feel the cool Atlantic air and to get her first taste of freedom in many years.

Pausing for a few brief minutes to speak to reporters, Jane responded to their questions. "It feels good," she said, as she stood on the courthouse steps. At that very moment, like a tidal bore, memories of Billy Stafford flooded back. For a brief time, she shook, as if someone's icy fingers had gone up her back. Then, she pushed the memories away. Those feelings of remorse would be better left for another day.

As she left, Jane passed a note to me, saying, "Take this, I know I can trust you to get it in the *The Advance* for me."

The neatly folded piece of paper was a message of gratitude. The note read, "I would like to thank all my friends and all you people who have supported me and helped me during my trial. Special thanks to a very fantastic guy, my lawyer, Alan Ferrier, and to Ruth Fox, Caroline Abbott, Rose Sampson and Dr. Dimock. Love goes out to all of my family and friends. Thanks also to Howie Pike and Archie Mason (RCMP officers who were involved with the investigation)."

The note was signed, "May God bless you all; Jane Stafford."

Saturday Night at
the Horseshoe

Typically, most rural towns in North America have at least one favourite hangout where locals congregate at the end of a busy week to unwind and forget about their troubles. Liverpool, Nova Scotia is no exception. In 1982, that favourite establishment was a rustic, but comfortable tavern called the Horseshoe located in the downtown area. It didn't matter to the locals that the western theme wasn't readily noticeable. All they cared about was having a place where they could meet friends, drink draft, and dance to the live bands.

On the Saturday night of November 20,1982, Jane (Stafford) Hurshman wanted to get out into the "real" world and be with some "normal" people for a change. After all, it had been many years since she could go out for the evening and not have to worry about getting beaten up when she came home. Following the turmoil of the recent trial, she wanted to relax and forget about her past. And she had reason to celebrate: earlier that day, the eleven-member Supreme Court jury had given her a new lease on life. Unfortunately, Jane would soon learn that the celebrity status which she had acquired during the course of her first-degree murder trial would not be easy to shake.

The Horseshoe was crowded as it was any night a live band was in town. As one might expect, the major topic of discussion was Jane (Stafford) Hurshman and it seemed everyone had their own opinion of what happened in that little house in Bangs Falls, about what Billy Stafford was "really" like, and about what should have happened to Jane earlier that day when her trial ended.

Some felt she should have been sent to jail because, no matter what the reason, she had taken the life of another human being. Others expressed views that Jane had already done her time. There was no middle ground in this debate—either you supported the jury's decision or you didn't.

It was about 9:30 p.m. when Jane and her sister Mona entered the tavern. Her presence caused an immediate stir in the smoke-filled room. Waves of whispers rippled through the capacity-filled tavern as the two women found a table in the centre of the room. Some were incensed that she would have the nerve to come out after everything that had happened. Others applauded Jane's quick move to re-establish some sanity in her life.

As the band played on and people drank more beer, most seemed to forget that Jane was in the room. There was an initial onslaught of people crowding around, hoping to have the chance to speak with the infamous woman dressed in jeans and a sweater. Once the novelty wore off, the people in the crowd returned to their own private gatherings. Occasionally, however, someone would go over to Jane's table and offer congratulations. If anyone said anything uncomplimentary that night, Jane didn't show it. In fact, she later said that everyone had been "very nice" to her and Mona that night.

Jane appeared to be tired, and for the most part, people gave her space. Just the same, Mona was very attentive in an effort to protect her sister from any adverse attention. Although I didn't really know what to say to her, I felt compelled to at least let her know I had seen her arrive. Much to my surprise, as I reached her table, I found myself asking Jane for a dance.

While we danced to a Beatles' medley, Jane admitted that she was finding all the attention somewhat unnerving. She seemed listless and paused frequently, almost as if fighting to keep from breaking under the stress. She was obviously struggling to appear normal, but the battle scars were evident.

"I don't like being looked at that way," she whispered in a soft voice, leaning forward to make herself heard over the loud music. "I'm not sure if I'll ever get used to all the attention."

By now Jane had been exposed to the human curiosity that all celebrities experience. She knew people wanted to talk with her about her ordeal, but she had trouble accepting the fact that she could command so much attention.

"It's hard to imagine that people would want to talk to me, because

I'm no different now than I was a few weeks ago; I'm still the same person I always was." However, she knew that because of the sensational trial, her life had changed forever and she appeared concerned about the loss of her privacy.

"I don't think things will ever be the same." She appeared frightened by that prospect, her voice breaking as she continued. "But I'm not trying to think about that tonight. I'd just like to forget all about that for awhile; that's one of the reasons I needed to get out," she explained, indicating that after the trial she needed to get her mind on other things. "It's been a long time since I didn't have to worry about Bill or going to court. But I didn't really know what to expect when I came in here."

She paused, almost withdrawing from the conversation. But then she pushed forward. "You know, it is sort of funny in a strange kind of way. I didn't really do anything that I should be famous for. I only did what I had to do. But I know some people think it was a big deal. I didn't do this to get famous or anything, but you and I know there are people who think that I did."

"I'm leaving town." She seemed saddened by this possibility, even though she had accepted the fact it was her only option. "I think the only way I can get away from everything and put it in the past is to get away from it all. I can't stay here; there's too many memories and too many things that remind me of what happened. I'm going to Ontario soon, but I hope we'll stay in touch."

We agreed that we would.

"Regardless of where I go, Queens County will always be my home, but I know I have to leave. It's too close to where everything happened and some people would never let me forget." She also knew her continued presence in the community would constantly remind Billy's family of the past.

"His people were good to me and I don't want to cause them any more pain, especially his mother and father. They've already suffered a lot because of the things that have come out." Visibly shaken, she continued, "I know there's a lot of people who don't believe everything that happened and I'll never be able to change their minds. But it was all the truth. We did live that way and that's a fact. I can't change my past and I can't change what I did. All I can do now is try to go ahead and make a new life for myself and my kids. I want them to have a normal life and I know there are people in this town who will never forgive me for what happened and that's one of the reasons I have to go."

When the song ended, Jane returned to her table where she continued to talk with those who stopped to wish her well. About ten minutes later, Jane and Mona began easing their way toward the exit. She waved across the room and I waved back—then she was gone.

Public Reaction: 'Making a Hero Out of a Murderer'

On December 2, 1982, Jane (Stafford) Hurshman, along with her two sons, Allen and Darren, left for Ontario, hoping to start a new life for themselves. Jane found out, however, that her hopes of finding a new life would quickly be dashed. Even as Jane and her boys were making plans to head for Ontario the wheels were in motion to appeal the not-guilty verdict.

Conversations about Jane (Stafford) Hurshman, Billy Stafford, and the murder trial became commonplace and widespread throughout the community of fewer than 14,000 residents. In fact, it seemed these were the favourite topics of discussion everywhere—schools, places of business, restaurants, the tavern, and the local bingo halls.

People understood the importance of this landmark trial, which represented the first time in Canadian legal history that the battered wife syndrome was used successfully as a defence. Despite that fact, local people resented the fact their privacy had been invaded and that there had been accusations made about numerous citizens who had lived and grown up in Queens County. Many reputations had been destroyed beyond repair and that did not sit well with some of the locals.

But the main problem hinged on a growing unease that Jane (Stafford) Hurshman was becoming a hero for killing another human being. It bothered people that instead of putting Jane on trial, the courts had actually tried Billy Stafford. They began to point out that the memory of Billy Stafford had been destroyed and that no one had defended him during the trial. In growing numbers, people were beginning to rethink their initial stand on this issue. Sure, they may have appreciated the fact that Jane could have been an abused wife, but did she have to kill Billy Stafford? Did Billy Stafford do all those horrible things that Jane claimed he did? Could she not have found another way out? It was these types of questions that seemed to be gnawing at people. The Crown was also rethinking its position and questioning whether justice had been served. Almost immediately following Jane's acquittal, it initiated procedures that would eventually see her return to the courtroom. Whenever the Crown loses a case, it is common practice to review the procedures: within weeks of the not-guilty verdict, the Nova Scotia Attorney General's office confirmed the trial tapes were being reviewed. Suspicions that the Crown would appeal the jury's verdict were growing more concrete.

Officials in the Attorney General's office conceded that if an appeal was made, it would not be on the jury's verdict as might have been expected, but on the auspices that an error in law had been made. In this case, it was felt that the judge had misinformed the jury on a point of law during the charge. In fact, officials stated, the judge should have informed the jury that the law of self-defence was never intended to excuse the killing of a defenceless, sleeping person.

On December 13, 1982, officials with the Attorney General's office issued notice to appeal the jury's verdict, and on December 15, they informed Jane, now living with her sister in Ontario, that an appeal had been launched.

For Jane, it meant the beginning of a new legal ordeal and, more importantly, that she would have to once again relive all those terrible memories. Her nightmarish life was starting all over again. During the second week of January 1983, she moved back to Queens County to deal with this new legal challenge to her freedom.

In a conversation shortly after her return from Ontario, Jane told me she did not want another long, drawn-out trial. "I want this to be over with. I want to get it behind me. I told them before that I would go to jail if they want me to, but let's get this settled once and for all because I just can't take it anymore." It was obvious that the strain of anticipating another trial was wearing on her; she appeared tired and frustrated.

"It just seems like this keeps going on and on. I can't believe that I'm going to have to go through all this again. Why didn't they just find me guilty in the first place and get it over with? I just go through it the first time and now they want me to do it all again but I just won't be able to make it; there's no way I can stand another drawn-out trial. Why don't they just send me to jail? That way, I'll at least know what's going on; I can't live like this anymore."

Despite this resurgence of emotions, Jane was not actually surprised by the Crown's move. It was no secret that almost everyone had been surprised at the jury's decision, including Blaine Allaby, the Crown Prosecutor. In a newspaper interview following the trial, Allaby said he believed Jane had been acquitted because of the evidence relating to the abuse she had allegedly suffered from the deceased, Billy Stafford. "I sort of thought it would have been reduced to manslaughter," he explained, but admitted he had not anticipated a not-guilty verdict.

Jane's lawyer Alan Ferrier said he too had been surprised at the verdict. In a February 1983 interview with *Globe and Mail* reporter Judy Steed, he pointed out the Crown went after Jane for first-degree murder, yet its own agents (RCMP officers) said on the witness stand she should get a medal for what she had done.

In that interview, Ferrier compared Jane's situation to that of a prisoner at Auschwitz who had been given the chance to kill her guard. He agreed his defence rested on evidence regarding Billy Stafford's abusive character and the suffering Jane had endured. The major thrust of his argument was toward a verdict of manslaughter but he did raise the possibility that the jury could find her not guilty on the grounds of self-defence.

The self-defence argument, which would become very important in the appeal decision, focused on the section of the Criminal Code of Canada titled Preventing Assault, which says "everyone is justified in using force to defend himself or anyone under this protection from assault if he uses no more force than is necessary to prevent the assault or the repetition of it."

In Steed's article, Ferrier argued, "In the context of being a prisoner, Mrs. Stafford was defending her son Allen (Whynot), who was under her protection. And I think we proved that she had nowhere to turn. Not even the police could cope with this guy. He was a bastard."

While some women's groups heralded the jury's verdict in the Stafford trial as a victory for battered women, Ferrier said he had a different opinion. "I don't see this verdict having consequences for other cases. Jury trials are not precedents for anything. But I think the verdict shows that our system of punishment isn't flexible enough to take into consideration abuse like this. By finding her not guilty, I think the jury was maybe telling the world that they didn't want this woman to be incarcerated for twenty-five years and perhaps not at all."

Initially, Ferrier pointed out, he had advised his client to plead guilty to manslaughter. This would have meant the punishment would be determined by the judge according to the circumstances of the case. But, without a doubt, she would have been sent to jail.

"She was prepared to go to jail for a couple of years," Ferrier told the *Globe and Mail*. "But the Attorney General's office evidently did not want to be seen to be engaging in plea bargaining on a murder trial and they made the decision to go for first-degree murder and to let the jury decide. Now they're not pleased with what the jury decided."

While once again there was a great deal of legal wrangling surrounding the trial and Jane's future, some public sentiment was on her side and there was a movement afoot to oppose the impending appeal. Jock Inglis, editor of *The Liverpool Advance*, wrote an opinion column titled "Justice is served" which pointedly illustrated the mood of some following Jane's acquittal on the first-degree murder charge late in 1982.

"The Supreme Court trial of Jane Marie Stafford ended with a not-guilty verdict. The community, while expecting a conviction of manslaughter, was generally supportive of the verdict. Even the RCMP officers when the verdict was given did not appear displeased by the outcome.

"The evidence heard by the eleven-person jury was extensive and thorough. The outcome of the trial would appear to indicate a giant step forward for the rights of women who suffer abuse at the hands of their mates. It would also suggest there are safeguards in our system—that our judicial system can, and does, make allowances for victims of abject abuse.

"Jane Stafford had lived in a prison of her own for the past several years. To incarcerate her would only have served to compound the wrong. Justice has been served."

In addition to this show of local support, rumour of the impending appeal had sparked a national debate which eventually found its way to Ottawa, where in the House of Commons Progressive Conservative MP Jennifer Cossit said she felt Jane Stafford was "more than justified in her actions and should not be punished by the law."

Cossit said Jane had been punished enough by her brutal husband, Billy Stafford. Plans by the Nova Scotia Attorney General's office to appeal her previous acquittal on first-degree murder charges were "horrendous," she said. In stressing her opposition to the appeal, the federal MP urged the justice minister of the day, Marck MacGuigan, to intervene to ensure Jane Stafford was not put through a second trial and that the not-guilty verdict be allowed to stand.

Cossit said she believed Jane had "already received enough punishment—five long years of painful mental and physical punishment—and it appears the Department of the Attorney General of Nova Scotia wants to punish her further. I believe this lady was more than justified in her actions to protect herself and her sons from this terrifying onslaught of repeated assault."

With speculation over a possible new trial running rampant across Canada, a letter-writing campaign was launched, most notably by Ontario citizens who condemned the Nova Scotia Department of the Attorney General for even considering an appeal.

One writer said in a letter to *The Liverpool Advance*, "How can the government even consider putting that woman on trial after everything she has already gone through. Surely, there must be some compassion for this woman who has lived in her own kind of hell for all these years. I think it's scandalous that the Attorney General's office is thinking about a new trial. All I can say is shame on you."

An editorial by Mildred Istona which appeared in the April 1983 issue of *Chatelaine*, one of Canada's leading magazines, put the debate into perspective when she said, "It is clear that, in the long run, there is no way to avoid the complexity of complex issues. As a society, we need to address issues with thoughtfulness and compassion."

Istona agreed that everyone is sickened by reports of wife abuse, but she asked if murder is ever an appropriate response. She noted when Jane Stafford was acquitted on first-degree murder charges, the courtroom had erupted in applause. Evidence from sixteen witnesses had portrayed Billy Stafford as a bully, heavy drinker and sexual sadist who had abused two previous wives and often beaten Jane unconscious.

But should the jury have found Jane (Stafford) Hurshman not guilty on the grounds of self-defence even after she had admitted killing her common-law husband, Billy Stafford in his sleep?

The Appeal

Although Jane (Stafford) Hurshman was not surprised that the Crown had launched an appeal process, she was becoming increasingly surprised and overwhelmed by the growing support she was receiving from across Canada, while in Queens County more and more people appeared to be turning away from her.

In 1983, while waiting to see what the outcome would be regarding the appeal, Jane revealed in a private conversation many personal thoughts about her situation. Although she had asked then that her comments be kept off the record, today, her words provide an insight into the woman that many people had never before seen. As we spoke on the telephone, she indicated that she was not only surprised by the increased local rejection, but also deeply hurt about how some locals were now treating her. She realized there would be people who would never believe her story, but she was not prepared for the open displays of resentment and even hatred that some her friends had displayed.

"It really bothers me," she said, "that some people would be like this. I know some people have a hard job believing everything that came out at the trial, but it was all true. What really hurts me is the way some people turn their backs to you. People that I thought were my friends won't even look at me now. I didn't do anything to these people but I wish they would try to understand that I really believed I had no other choice."

As she continued, she expressed remorse that she had brought so much attention to her hometown and disrupted the lives of so many

As Jane (Stafford) Hurshman looked in July 1983 when she was one of 16 students to complete a 14-week Job Readiness Training program sponsored by the Canada Employment Centre.

people who had been her friends. "I didn't mean these people any harm; it's just that I didn't know what else to do. I didn't know there were places I could go and even the police were scared of him. How do you think you would feel when big policemen were afraid of this guy? You'd be scared too."

Pausing to carefully select her words, she added, "I was afraid of Bill because he hurt me really bad and he had killed before. I knew he was going to kill me some day. I knew that it was either going to be me or him that got killed in that house and I didn't want it to be me. I didn't really care about myself but I didn't want to leave my kids with him; he would have killed them too."

In fact, Jane said that on the night of March 11,1982, she considered killing herself as well. "There was a minute when I thought I should shoot myself too, but I thought better of that because I had to get the yard cleaned up before Darren saw anything. I thought about shooting myself because I knew everything that happened with Bill would come out in court and that would hurt my kids real bad."

However, she quickly added, "I thought better of that because I didn't want to leave my kids alone after everything they went though. They needed me and I needed them."

As she waited to see what would happen next, Jane prepared for the worst. She expected the appeal to go through and accepted the inevitability of a jail sentence. She just wanted the ordeal to be over. "I just can't cope with this," she said. "I wish it was all over and they'd send me to jail if that's what they want."

By the fall of 1983, Crown lawyers were back in court before the Nova Scotia Supreme Court appeals division seeking a new trial for Jane Stafford.

In a twenty-eight-page written decision, handed down on November 30, 1983, a five-judge appeal court panel overturned the not-guilty verdict from the first trial when it unanimously concluded the judge at the original trial had misdirected the jury on a number of points of law. Justice J.A. Hart explained that these points were errors made by the trial judge as to the defence of justification, which may have misdirected the jury.

One somewhat dubious case in point occurred when the trial judge incorrectly informed the jury that drunkenness was a complete defence of justification, rather than simply a means of reducing a conviction of murder to one of manslaughter. Obviously, this point of law had little to do with the case in question: drunkenness had never been introduced in Jane's defence (she had testified she had had nothing to drink the night of the shooting). Justice Hart said that, in his opinion, "there was not factual basis to support the alleged defence and the matter should not have been placed before the jury at all." He added, however, that it was difficult to determine if this particular error would have affected the verdict.

More relevant to the case was the question of whether the jury had been improperly directed with regard to the defence of justification pursuant to Section 37 of the Criminal Code.

Justice Hart pointed out that while the facts of the matter before the jury were not complicated, there was a great deal of evidence presented to indicate the terrible circumstances under which Jane had been living with Billy Stafford in the years since the birth of their only son, Darren. Although this evidence was obviously admitted in an attempt to establish a certain state of mind as it related to the defence of provocation at the time Jane Stafford pulled the trigger, the question remained if any or all of the evidence should have been admitted in the first place to be debated and discussed by legal experts.

The theory of the defence, as explained to the jury by the presiding judge, was that Jane shot Billy "on the sudden impulse and before there was time for her passions to cool as a result of threats of arson to Margaret Joudrey and a threat to deal with her son Allen. Such threats in the submission for the accused amounted to provocation. It is the further theory of the defence that the accused shot Mr. Stafford in the reasonable belief that Mr. Stafford was going to assault her son Allen and that such force was necessary."

Problems arose when the trial judge, Justice C.D. Burchell, instructed the jury on the specific indictment of first-degree murder, emphasizing that in order to find the defendant guilty of this crime, the question of intent had to be established beyond a reasonable doubt.

Justice Hart pointed out that Justice Burchell told the jury "that there were a number of defences that had to be considered," including those of insanity and drunkenness, and particularly the matter of provocation and the question of self-defence.

Justice Hart noted that Justice Burchell had explained that in order to find Jane (Stafford) Hurshman not guilty with defence, there was no burden on the accused to prove that she had acted in self-defence. Instead, the burden was on the Crown to prove beyond a reasonable doubt that the accused had not acted in self-defence. The fact that Billy Stafford was asleep when he was shot played an important part in this argument.

Hart also charged that Justice Burchell spent five of his seven-hour instruction to the jury, "reiterating evidence given by witnesses during the trial," (the main portion of which focused on the character of the deceased) rather than simply, "relating certain parts of the evidence to the principles of law which the judge had been explaining." Hart seemed to agree with much of the community that it was really Billy who had been on trial, and claimed that much of this evidence "was unnecessary and, indeed, inadmissible unless it was relevant to a defence that could properly be put to the jury. It served only to create sympathy for the respondent and for this reason should have been excluded."

After the completion of the final instructions from the judge, the jury had retired to deliberate and returned a not-guilty verdict. "It is from this verdict that the Crown has appealed," Justice Hart said, explaining that the only route by which the jury could have arrived at its conclusion "was if they understood from the judge's instructions that Section 37 of the Criminal Code permitted Jane Stafford to anticipate a possible assault against her son from threats made earlier in the evening and that she used reasonable force to prevent such an assault."

Although the jury had been given a copy of Section 37, he said, "the legal definition of assault was not placed before them and the jury might well have understood that threats alone could amount to an assault."

However, he pointed out, the Criminal Code is clear in this regard. "A person who seeks justification from preventing an assault against himself or someone under his protection must be faced with an actual assault, something that he must defend against, before the provisions of Section 37 can be invoked. The assault must be life-threatening before he can be justified in killing in defence of his person or that of someone under his protection."

At the time that Jane Stafford said she shot and killed Billy Stafford, he was sleeping in the truck. Justice Hart responded, "There was no assault against her and only a general statement during the evening that he would deal with Allen. Allen was the only person who could be said to be under her protection and there is no evidence that Billy Stafford was about to assault him at the time he was killed."

Justice Hart said he did not believe that the trial judge, Justice Burchell, was justified in placing Section 37 of the Criminal Code before the jury. Under Section 37, he explained, the assault must be such that it is necessary to defend the person assaulted by the use of force. "No more force may be used than necessary to prevent the assault or the repetition of it. Nobody was being assaulted at the time Billy Stafford was killed. There was not need to protect anybody from any assault," Justice Hart explained, pointing out the deceased was not even awake at the time of the shooting. "In my opinion, no person has the right, in anticipation of an assault that may or may not happen, to apply force to prevent the imaginary assault. The jury should not have been permitted to consider a possible assault as a justification to her deed, and Section 37 of the Criminal Code should not have been left with them."

In light of those facts the five-member appeal court found the jury had been improperly instructed on the law relating to the offence, which permitted its members to reach a conclusion that would not otherwise be open to them. The court allowed the Crown's appeal, set aside the not-guilty verdict of the jury and ordered a new trial upon the original indictment of first-degree murder.

For Jane (Stafford) Hurshman, this decision meant the beginning of another grueling and emotionally taxing chapter in her life. Now, the appeal court was saying she wasn't justified in her actions because there was no immediate threat to herself or her son Allen and that the assaults he had bragged about on the night he died may have only been imagined.

However, for Jane the threats were as real as the physical and emotional abuse she had endured. Commenting on the appeal, Jane said, "That's their decision and I can't change how they feel or how they see things. To me those threats were real and I know he would have hurt Margaret and Allen that night if I hadn't stopped him."

In her mind, she was free of the pain she had suffered from Billy Stafford and it did not matter that the appeal court may not have been able to fully understand or appreciate the kind of life she had lived. "Sometimes, I wonder what these people would do if they were faced with the things we took from Bill?"

Happy Valentine's Day

Tuesday, February 14, 1984, Valentine's Day, almost two years after the death of Billy Stafford, was judgment day for Jane (Stafford) Hurshman.

In the days leading up to February 14, Jane spent as much time as possible with her family, particularly her children. She had no idea what the outcome of the trial would be, or what the future held for her. Jane knew, as did her family and supporters, that she could be looking at a long jail term if the court decided to be particularly tough on her, and she used the time beforehand to take care of business and tie up loose ends. Everything was in place so that if she had to spend any length of time in jail, her children would be looked after.

She wasn't afraid to go back to court, she said bravely from her home in Bangs Falls in a telephone conversation that had taken place a few days earlier. Even though the house held painful memories, Jane felt she had no alternative but to reside there until her future was determined by the courts. "I don't care how long they send me to jail for, it can't be any worse than the prison I was already living in."

Admittedly, though, she was nervous of the unknown. "I'm not afraid of what will happen to me, but I don't like the idea of being so far away from my family without any contact and I'm afraid for my kids. I'm not looking forward to going to jail, but at least this will be over; that's one good thing about all of this."

Trying to appear strong, Jane asked what the public mood in Queens County was concerning the new trial. It was a tough call, but I suggested to her that the community was split about fifty-fifty. However, I noted, most people agreed the Crown should have entered into a plea bargain before the first trial, as the defence had wanted, instead of giving her the chance to be found not guilty. That would have prevented all this legal horseplay.

Jane responded bitterly, "These people don't know the half of it. There was a lot more that I could have said about Bill, but it wasn't necessary. I still can't believe that so many people think I wanted to live like that. It really makes me sick to think that some people would think I would ask to be treated worse than a dog. And as far as leaving goes, it's fine to say leave him, but unless you're in the situation, you don't know what you're talking about."

"When you're afraid of someone like I was of Bill, you don't just pick up and leave. It ain't that easy," she said. "And, you know, you almost begin to blame yourself for the kind of mess you got yourself into. After you hear something enough, you begin to believe it. When you're always told it was all your fault or that you ain't no good for nothing over and over, you begin to think that's the truth."

She paused for a few seconds to gather her thoughts and then quickly added, "But if I learned anything about all of this, it's that I shouldn't have kept quiet about what was going on. I should have told somebody and I hope others find a way out so they don't have to do what I did." In the nearly two years since she shot Billy Stafford, Jane had come to learn that she was not alone, but in fact was only one of thousands of women who are being abused every day in Canada.

As I hung up the telephone receiver, I thought about the conversation I had just had with the woman who was sparking a nation-wide debate on the issue of wife battering. I remember thinking how strange it was that this woman, who with one gunshot had taken the fight against domestic violence leap years into the future, would still be a victim of a system that is designed to protect the abuser and not the victim.

Year after year in Canada, there are horror stories of abused women killing their spouses because they see no other way out of a system that makes it possible for the perpetrator to continue his life in the comfort of his own home, while the battered woman and her children have to flee in search of a safe place to hide. More shocking still are the statistics of the number of women who are killed each year in this country by an abusive husband or boyfriend.

The system fails these victims of abuse because it urges the family to reconcile and therefore the woman remains within reach of her abuser. In many instances, although these victims may have sought legal help for fear of their own safety, the system does not provide ample protection and the case becomes another tragic statistic. Society fails to recognize that when a woman says she is afraid of her mate or feels threatened by her partner, she has good reason. It was that kind of attitude that prevailed when Jane was being abused and, as a result, she kept her painful secrets inside until, like a caged animal, she fought back.

As February 14 drew near, Jane was coming to terms with the reality of her predicament. To a certain extent she was relieved because she knew that at the end of the day's court proceedings, her legal battles would be over. However, her emotional struggles would continue for the rest of her life. In court that day, Jane Marie (Stafford) Hurshman pleaded guilty to a reduced charge of manslaughter and was sentenced in Supreme Court, held at the Liverpool courthouse, to six months confinement in a provincial institution to be followed by two years of probation. The presiding judge, Justice Merlin Nunn, also allowed Jane to leave the institution to attend classes at vocational school in Bridgewater on the condition that she return to jail each evening.

Ironically, this was the same reduced charge that Jane's defence lawyer had wanted prior to the first trial. Fortunately the second trial ended quickly and for Jane that meant she did not have to endure another drawn out affair.

During the proceedings, Blaine Allaby, the Crown Prosecutor, said in reference to an upgrading program that Jane had completed in 1983, that the pre-sentence report was favourable and spoke well of her efforts to start a new life. He noted that although Jane had obviously gone through considerable problems, she appeared to have made many improvements in her life, especially in her efforts to upgrade her education. He said that a period of incarceration in a provincial institution, with consideration for educational needs, would be considered appropriate by the Crown.

Jane's lawyer, Alan Ferrier, in urging the court to be lenient in its punishment, stressed the severe physical and sexual abuse she had suffered. He placed great emphasis on the fact that she did not pose a threat to the community and had shown great courage in improving her personal conditions since the time of the offence. During his forty-five-minute address to the court, Ferrier referred several times to the jury

Jane (Stafford) Hurshman looked downcast and withdrawn after the second trial found her guilty of manslaughter on February 14, 1984.

decision in the earliest trial, saying it reflected the community's feelings on Jane's case.

Standing beside Ferrier, the man in whom she had placed so much trust over the past two years, Jane listened intently to Justice Nunn. Before imposing the sentence, the judge said it was apparent that much of Jane's life had been a tragedy and most of it had been lived in fear. He pointed out, however, that on the night of March 11, 1982, Jane became judge, jury and executioner at once, and he said, "Human life is not to be snuffed out at will and she should have sought other means to extricate herself and her family from the situation."

Finally, when Jane had steadied herself for the worst, Justice Nunn turned the tide by pointing to the progress she had made in putting her life in order and said he did not feel she was a danger to society. On the other hand, a suspended sentence would not serve as a deterrent to society and so he gave her a six-month conditional term of imprisonment.

Jane's supporters applauded the sentence, pointing out that incarcerating this woman for a long period of time would have served no purpose. And although these individuals and groups felt the appeal never should have been allowed in the first place, they found in Jane Hurshman a person who symbolized the plight of the abused woman; they had found their hero and in the years that followed they would use her, time and time again, to mount a campaign to fight the injustices battered women endure.

In an editorial which appeared in the February 22, 1984, issue of *The Advance*, publisher Jock Inglis summed up what he felt was the public mood in the wake of the second trial and Jane's subsequent jail sentence. He wrote, "the people of Queen's County appear to be reluctantly content with the outcome of the murder trial of Jane Marie Stafford. The Crown, for its part, appears to be at rest, now that she has received punishment for her crime."

He continued, "Jane Stafford had been innocent in the eyes of her peers, a duly constituted group of Queen's County citizens who, after listening to the evidence presented by the Crown and the defence, found her not guilty of the charge.... There are those of us who felt that the jury was the pillar of our judicial system, that once we are found to be innocent by a group of our fellow citizens, we are free to go about our business. We know now that is not so.... Yes, the Crown got its pound of flesh through her incarceration, but at what cost to our justice system?"

However, while a certain faction recognized Jane's case as an opportunity to underscore the tragedy of domestic violence, there is still a large group highly agitated over the leniency of the court. It was difficult for some to get beyond the fact that this woman was becoming a hero for killing another human being in cold blood.

But regardless of which side of the fence the public was on, the bottom line was that Jane was going to jail. She had come to terms with what she had done and accepted the reality of the situation a long time ago. On that day in the Liverpool courthouse when she heard the sentence, she was prepared to go to jail. Steeling herself as the sentence was handed down, she breathed deeply and then relaxed. At long last, it was over.

Behind Bars

By now, Jane (Stafford) Hurshman had become resigned to the fact that going to jail was part of her fate. To her, it was just another place to live and she was prepared to make the most of it. During the nearly two-hour drive in the sheriff's car from the Liverpool courthouse to the Halifax Correctional Centre on February 14, her past flooded back like a dam had broken: the abuse, the night she shot Billy, the trials, her children. Life, she realized, was cruel and good at the same time. She would survive the time in jail by immersing herself in her studies. Prior to this court appearance, Jane had enrolled in a certified nursing assistant's course and she was relieved the judge had made it possible for her to continue.

It was mid-afternoon when the car pulled up in front of the desolate grey building that, for the next few months, would separate her from the free world. After being processed and given standard prison clothing, Jane was taken to her cold, six-by-eight-foot cell. The walls closed around her as the bars clanged shut. There wasn't much in the cell—a steel bed, a sink, and a toilet. Meals were delivered on a metal tray and although there was no privacy, the isolation she felt behind the bars was nearly unbearable. She was kept in her own cell for four days before being introduced to the prison's general population.

On her first night in prison, Jane encountered other inmates who tried to present tough first impressions. Some of these women had been sentenced to long jail terms for shooting their mates and were not impressed that Jane had only been given six months for the same offence. Jane learned quickly that in prison things are not always what they seem and she put up her own wall. If she was going to survive in jail, she knew she could not appear weak. With that attitude, she was able to fit in with the other prisoners.

Eventually, she was moved from her own cell to one of two dormitories in the women's block. In total, there were about twenty women in this section of the prison. There, where she could talk to other people, life in prison got better for Jane. Her studies also made it easier to cope. She got up at 6 a.m. each day and drove her own car to school.

The days of travelling between Halifax and Bridgewater to attend classes at the Lunenburg Vocational School (now the South Shore Community College) were difficult, but Jane remained committed to her goal and used those hours on the road to think about her future. Memories of her past constantly pushed their way to the surface on her long drives, but she felt they would eventually subside and was determined to complete her studies. The driving force behind her aspirations was the desire to start a new life for both herself and her sons.

Although Jane only served one-third of her six-month jail term, those two months were "like a living hell, but I got by. Before all this happened, I never ever thought I'd be behind bars, but I know it was necessary." Jane liked to write, often committing her deepest feelings to paper. It was that outlet that allowed Jane to come to terms with the emotions that surfaced behind the prison bars.

Only two days after her incarceration on February 16, Jane wrote in response to my letter asking for an interview:

> *Dear Vernon,*
>
> *I received your letter today and I was quite pleased to hear from you. The trial is over and I am glad. After practically living with all you people in the courtroom for three weeks of my life, and it being a very critical period for me, I did consider you a friend at that time and still do.*
>
> *When I left the courtroom that day, I never kept any contact with most people, not due to any fault of any of you, but due to the fact that at that time I didn't feel good enough to be in the company of "decent" people.*
>
> *I have come a long way since then Vernon, with the help of professionals, friends and myself and with the hope for a new future.*

I realize now it was a terrible way to look at things, but I am still learning how to deal with myself and with my emotions, and I pray that during my lifetime I never stop learning. The world is beautiful and there are good people out there, but I have to give them a chance, as well as myself.

Anytime you wish to drop in on me at school, well feel free to do so. My noon hour is from 11:40 until 12:20 and I eat in the school cafeteria. I do look forward to your visit because even though some reporters can be cruel, I have never considered you to be cruel or heartless to me. You did an excellent job in reporting my case and I appreciate that.

The fact of my spending time in "this place" (jail), well, I do accept the fact that I am here and I consider myself to be very fortunate.

I will be looking forward to seeing you. You can call the school and leave a message if you plan to visit me and I can meet you at the front doors of the school.

> *Thanks for being a friend*
> *Jane Stafford*

The arrangements were made and a few days later I was on my way from Liverpool to meet with Jane. I was nervous about the interview but the half-hour drive to Bridgewater provided me with time for reflection.

Arriving at the vocational school just before noon, I found Jane waiting for me at the front doors just as she had promised. It was a cold day and although she said she had not been waiting long, she was noticeably shivering as we shook hands. Her grip was icy, but her smile was warm and friendly. After chatting for a few moments, it was time to get down to business.

Before starting, she consented to answer any questions but asked if I could dispense with taking notes. "I'd just like to talk as friends. I trust you to get it right without using notes. It's been awhile since I talked to someone other than my family and I'd just like to talk."

Not waiting for a response, she suggested we take a walk, and turned down one of the school's long corridors. We walked silently for a few minutes. Sensing my uneasiness, Jane paused and leaned against the brick wall. "I know you want a story and you can write about anything you want. It just seems so formal when you take notes."

Breathing deeply, and with downcast eyes, she explained she still felt uneasy about talking with reporters, even ones she trusted. She seemed reluctant to talk at all. However, after regaining her usual composure, she began by describing her life in prison.

"I'm not complaining about being in there, but prison is still prison regardless if you're fortunate to have the kind of the privileges that I have and that's all there is to it. If you have never been to jail, you have no idea what it's like. There's no way you could ever be prepared for that kind of life, regardless of how much you know it's the right thing." Acknowledging that her day passes did provide her some connection with the outside world, she still insisted, "It's hard to give up your freedom and go back there every day. I thought I could handle it, but there's no substitute to being able to come and go as you please. When they lock me up, it's like nothing you can imagine. You feel like a caged animal: you have no freedoms; someone else tells you what to do."

She paused, looking wishful, and then let down her guard, "I wish it was all over. The guards are nice and some of the other women are good to get along with, but it isn't the same as being able to come and go as you want. I know it's only a few months, but it seems like a long time. I just want to be home with my kids."

She began fiddling with a button on her beige shirt sleeve, which seemed to be annoying her. She was dressed simply that day—blue slacks and a plain shirt. There was nothing phony about this woman, and although she seemed somewhat pensive, she spoke with sincerity. She explained that one of the ways she handled the trauma of prison life was to write. "I like poetry. Writing makes me feel good, because it helps me to get away from it all."

When she wasn't writing poetry or letters, she lost herself in school work. "I study a lot," she said proudly. "And having my parents for company every day at lunch is also good for me." She had requested only a few visitors during her time in jail.

But it was those long, dark hours between the time when the prison lights went out and dawn that were the most difficult to deal with. "I often wish nighttime would never come." She hesitated, squeezing her eyelids tightly shut, "Night brings the nightmares. I know that's all over now, but I can't stop the memories. Sometimes, I dream about March 11, four or five times a night; I don't think there's a night that goes by that I don't think about that. They're only dreams and I know they can't hurt me, but they seem so real; it's almost like I can still feel him kicking and punching me. I don't know if the memories will ever go away."

She turned, and walked away. I gave her a few minutes to compose herself and then cautiously asked if there were any specific incidents of abuse that she recalled above the others. There was silence. I was about to apologize when she began to speak in a whispered monotone.

"There were so many times that they all seem to run together into one," Jane said, turning to face me. There was real terror in her eyes. Even though Billy Stafford was gone, he still had a grip on her. Her eyes were round and glassy and she didn't blink. Her look was sharp, almost as if she was staring right through me. "He did so much to me and the kids that I couldn't begin to tell you which was the worst.

"I think I remember more about how stupid and insignificant he made me feel, even more than the physical pain. When you tell someone over and over how stupid and ugly they are, they begin to believe it. Bill was a mean, cruel person and I can't make you really see what he was like. You'd have to get to know him like he really was before you could understand."

If she could change anything about her life with Billy Stafford or the night of March 11, 1982 she said, matter-of-factly, she would never have gotten involved with him in the first place.

"If I knew what he was like, I would never have gone with him," Jane replied. "Even after he started hitting me, I should have left him; I should have found some way out, but I didn't. I don't have any regrets about what I did that night, except that I shouldn't have gotten Allen involved. I really felt for him because he went through so much and took a lot off of people. I'm sorry that I blamed him at first for killing Bill. I know that was wrong and I'll never forgive myself for it. I love my children and I would never do anything to hurt them; I just wish he hadn't been there that night to get me the gun."

Shooting Billy was the only way she knew to escape his torture, Jane explained, bracing herself once again against the brick wall of the corridor. "Once I put the gun through that window, there was no turning back for me. I knew what I had to do. I am sorry that it came to that, but I'm not sorry Bill is dead. The way I figure, it would have either been him or me."

Our time together was running out, so I turned the conversation to her studies, which she assured me were going well. "I like this. It's something I always wanted to do," she said, and agreed that studying to be a nursing assistant was good therapy. "I want to help people and this will be a good way."

Jane explained that she had been scheduled to do her on-the-job training at Queens General Hospital in Liverpool, but she decided it would be best if she did not return to Queens County at that time, so she arranged to switch with another student. She completed her practical work at the Fisherman's Memorial Hospital, in Lunenburg, which, conveniently for her, was closer to Halifax than Liverpool. "I'm not ready to come back home just yet. I know things will never be the same there and I don't think I'll be able to come back there again to live. People can be very cruel and I know what some people are saying about me, but I can't deal with that right now so the best thing to do is just not to go there."

Once she completed her jail term and after graduation that spring, she was leaving the South Shore and possibly even Nova Scotia. She thought she might try living in Ontario again. "I'd like to stay closer to home, but I know things will never be normal again, so I think it's best for me and the boys if we just move far, far away."

The large clock on the school wall reminded Jane there were only minutes before her classes were to resume. Walking back to the school's main entrance, she commented how fast the time had gone.

As we reached the door, seeming forceful and more in control of herself, Jane insisted that she was slowly getting her life back to normal and that when she got out of jail, she would put her past behind her.

Wrapping her long arms about her gaunt frame to fight the cold air blowing through an open door and down the hall, she exclaimed, "I want to spend as much time with my kids as I can because I've missed so much of their lives, if you can call what they had with Bill a life. But all that's going to change now."

I nodded in agreement, but wondered aloud if she would ever be able to forget. She hesitated a moment, then replied, "I'm not sure if I'll really get over what Bill did to me, but I'm going to try. I know that I can make a different life for myself and my kids and that's all I'm going to concentrate on. I'm going to get a good job when I finish school and try to put Bill behind me; it won't be easy, but I'm going to give it a good try."

Our conversation was over.

As she put her back to the large glass door, she smiled and thanked me. "I trust you," she said, "I just needed someone other than my family to talk to." Leaving the school, I turned to wave, but Jane was gone. Her quick disappearance seemed somehow appropriate. The frail woman who had momentarily opened up her heart to me had retreated into the sanctuary that the school provided. No one was going to hurt her anymore. Nevertheless, it was the painful memories that she was running from now and from those there was nowhere to hide.

Throughout February and March, Jane continued to drive to Bridgewater every day to continue her studies. And every day, her parents, Maurice and Gladys Hurshman, would drive from Queens County to have lunch with their daughter. Often, they brought along someone else to visit with Jane, usually one of her children. It was that continuous contact with the outside world that provided some form of normality to Jane's life and gave her the strength to carry on.

However, even as Jane tried to carve out a new niche in life, the publicity surrounding the death of Billy Stafford persisted. In an issue dated March 21, 1984, *The Advance* published a letter written by Billy Stafford's father. It read:

> *Dear sir:*
>
> *Two years ago this month, my son was murdered. He left behind a mother, father, sisters, and brothers. On March 13, the ghouls on CBC's* Fifth Estate *saw fit to crucify him again.*
>
> *Ronald Wamboldt and Allen Whynot lived at my son's getting free room and board. They came to my house two or three times a week and I made a number of trips to their home at Bangs Falls. For all the physical abuse they were supposed to have taken from my son, I never saw a mark on either of them. I never saw any of them tied so they could not leave when they felt like it. I do not know of anyone my son had murdered or why the police think they had to go there armed.*
>
> *My son was on boats for years and he never had any trouble, to my knowledge. It is all very well to give statements in court and to the newspaper when the one person who could deny them is dead and apparently there was no one to verify them.*

*The many people who could have been called to testify on
his behalf were never summoned by the Crown. If anyone
takes offense at these remarks, they know where to get in
contact with me, Billy's father.*

Lamonte Stafford

Jane had always enjoyed receiving *The Advance* each week during
her time at the correctional center. It was like a letter from home with
all the local news and social notes. However, on this particular day, she
was forced to confront her deep feelings of sorrow and remorse for the
family of Billy Stafford. Jane suddenly realized, with deep regret, that
in defending her actions she had destroyed the fond memories Billy
Stafford's family—in particular his mother and father—had had of him.

After reading Lamonte Stafford's letter Jane wept. All the abuse she
had suffered from Billy seemed to be forgotten. "I cried a lot that night,"
she later recalled. "I couldn't get those feelings out of my mind about
what I had done to Bill's father. I kept thinking about how his mother
and father must have felt and I could understand how upset all of this
must have made them. I didn't wish his family any harm and I regret any
pain I may have caused them."

The words of Billy's father had made an impression. Again, I wrote
to ask her for another interview but her reply was elusive:

March 23, 1984

Dear Vernon,

*At this point, I really do not wish to do another interview,
no offense or anything. It's just that since court on February
14, I am just now starting to get some order in my life and I
am trying so very hard to put my past where it belongs, in the
past. It seems I just get that accomplished and then it is all
in front of me again and you know each time I have to go
through it, you would think it gets easier, but really it
doesn't; it gets harder.*

*Also Vernon, I read Lamonte's piece that was published
this week and I wish no more hurt or bad feelings to him. He
is a fine man and I respect him very much, but he has suffered
dearly and I choose not to have anymore printed, even if only*

for that reason. He is a man that has been good to me over the years and I just want to let my past rest now.

I do hope that you understand my reasoning. I am sorry if I have caused you any inconvenience. If, when I get out of here and you wish to visit me at home, feel free to do so. You are welcome.

Admittedly, her reluctance to respond to Lamonte's public statement caught me off guard, but I accepted and respected her reasons. I had not yet published the article based on our previous conversation at the vocational school in Bridgewater. That article was never published, and her comments were kept in confidence, until now.

On April 14, 1984, Jane became eligible for parole, and in June she graduated from the Lunenburg Vocational School as a fully-qualified nursing assistant. She was ready to face the world; a world she could enter for the first time in many years as a free woman.

Starting Over

The facts are that in Canada, one in four women will be victims of sexual assault at some time in their lives; as many as one in six women are abused in their own homes; 62 per cent of all women murdered are victims of domestic violence; 90 per cent of sexual assault victims are women while 99 per cent of the perpetrators are men; 80 per cent of the women in federal prisons have a history of being physically or sexually abused; every fifteen seconds a wife is beaten by her spousal partner. Furthermore, in 1990-91, two women a month were murdered in Canada by their partner or ex-partner. These are shocking statistics and they underline the seriousness of a problem that will continue to grow unless society accepts the truth and deals with it.

Jane Hurshman's relationship with Billy Stafford made her one of these statistics and it was the tragic circumstances of her own experience that eventually lead her to speak out about wife abuse and domestic violence.

On April 14, 1984, Jane was paroled from the Halifax County Correctional Centre. She would remain on probation until August 14, 1986. Despite her new-found freedom, it was the lingering memories of her life with Billy that would continue to torment her in the years that followed. Upon her graduation later that year from the Lunenburg Vocational School, Jane was accepted for a job at the Halifax County Regional Rehabilitation Centre. Initially, she turned down the job. Wanting to put the events of her past behind her, she thought a different location away from the memories would give her a new beginning. She and her boys moved to Toronto to live with her sister. Eventually, though, the need to be near her family and the desire to work in her field pulled her back to Nova Scotia. Within a few months, she returned to Halifax and took the job she had been offered there, where she remained for eight years.

In the years following her trials and jail term, Jane became a highly visible personality in Nova Scotia by speaking out against domestic violence and telling other victims that they can escape abusive relationships. As a survivor, she hoped to set an example for other women in similar situations, and to show other women that they do not have to let it happen to them. She wanted other victims of abuse to know they don't have to be ashamed or fearful about seeking help; she wanted them to know they are not alone.

In her public presentations, Jane attempted to help other victims realize that women who are being abused are often lulled into thinking that the situation will get better, or they are made to believe the situation is their own fault. She said, "After all, their husband loves them, and they love their husband. But what these women fail to understand is that the situation will never improve and that they are not to blame for the abuse they are suffering."

Jane was a strong voice because she knew how the abusive husband thinks. "In most cases, spousal partners who abuse their mate do so out of a need to be in control. He may love his wife and she may love him in return, but the abuse is real as his insecurity has led him into commiting violent acts against the person he most dearly loves. The bottom line is that the man who batters feels that if he can control the woman, he can control his own fears."

She used her own life with Billy Stafford to illustrate the point and she believed because of the extreme violence she endured, her message would reach other battered women, and maybe even other members of society. Perhaps, she thought, she could make a difference. Jane knew that what many people fail to understand about the issue of domestic abuse is that violence does not only mean physical force. In fact, any act, whether it be physical or verbal, that does not allow someone to act on their own, is violence. Even isolation and economic abuse against women, which is especially predominant in rural communities, is considered violence.

As real as this abuse is, society does not recognize these acts as violence and Jane knew it was this type of ingrained thinking that supports the battered woman's decision to stay in her abusive relationship. "It is not unusual for an abused woman to ask herself what will the family say or what will the neighbours think if she leaves her husband," she claimed. It was this conditioning, along with the fear, that kept Jane with her abusive mate for five years. However, by 1985, she was beginning to learn that she could be a valuable soldier in the war against domestic violence.

Being an advocate against domestic violence was a role Jane would play for many years; it was a role into which she threw her heart and soul, despite the personal toll it may have been taking. She believed that violence against women must be dealt with as a social, rather than as a women's issue and she worked hard to get her message out to as many people as would listen.

Jane loved her work as a nursing assistant, but it was her eventual role as a spokesperson against domestic violence and wife abuse that provided her with her motivation. By the end of 1984, only a few months after her parole, she was already being called upon to speak at public functions about her life with Billy Stafford.

In December that year, Jane wrote in a letter, "It is true that time is a healing element—and in my case, that's true because I am finding it all much easier to deal with and talk about [my situation]. I have been asked to attend a workshop for women's and children's crisis. I am considering doing that as it will be held in either Queens or Lunenburg County and it is a two-day affair. Something like that interests me because there is a possibility that I can reach some other woman or child who is living that life and let them know there is help available without going to the limits that I did."

Jane did attend that workshop at the Oak Island Inn, a comfortable resort near Chester. It was March 1985 and this was her first public appearance. She spoke with feeling from a victim's perspective. She wasn't an eloquent speaker, but she touched everyone with the sincerity of her words. It was then that she first assumed her position as a highly visible opponent of wife battering and crimes against women. By this time, Jane had come to realize there was no escape from her past, that indeed, because of the publicity surrounding her life and trials, many people expected her to be their symbol for the fight against domestic violence; she was their hero.

However, as one of her closest friends points out, she did not resent that role, but instead accepted the reality of the situation and used it to help others. Wendy Annand, a parole officer with Correctional Services Canada under the umbrella of the Department of Solicitor General, got to know Jane while she was on parole and, discovering they shared many of the same experiences, the two became very close friends. It was Annand who invited Jane to speak at her first workshop at the Oak Island Inn.

She remembers that while still in the middle of attempting to put her life back together, "Jane started to get a sense of her new position. She began to realize that people, especially other abused women, were looking to her for help."

Soon, Annand points out, Jane came to realize she could use this position to help others. "And she did," she adds, explaining she believed it was Jane's objective to give people an understanding of how a battered woman lives and to inform victims of abuse that there is help available.

"First and foremost, Jane was a survivor and that was the image she wanted to portray," her friend continues. "She was a good example of an abused woman who lived through years of hell, but eventually found a way out. Although she chose a route most would not have taken, she showed other victims that life can go on."

Despite the public attention Jane commanded where she spoke, she never pretended to be something she wasn't. According to Annand, "She lived by the motto that her past had happened, that she was able to get away from her abuser and that she was a survivor. Her desire was to help others do the same."

Meanwhile, as Jane was starting out on her campaign against domestic violence, controversy erupted back home following the August 13, 1985 meeting of Queens Municipal Council when councillors refused to give $6400 to support a transition house being proposed for Lunenburg and Queens County. If there had been such a facility in place when she was being abused, Billy may still have been alive. Much to some people's surprise, the public outrage at the council's decision was immediate and loud when six of the eleven councillors attending the regular monthly meeting said they felt a local transition house was not needed and that a request for such funding would place an added burden on the county.

Indeed, it may not have been the decision itself which raised the public's ire, but rather the attitude of some councillors during debate on the issue, who publicly embarrassed Queens County in the process. The public was incensed by the blatant disregard for women that was shown by some councillors.

One male councillor said he could not see any need for such a facility and added that in a number of cases the availability of such facilities only creates additional problems. He also said that because of the advertising campaigns these facilities conduct, "They become almost a vacation spot for some women and entice the women to leave their homes and families."

Another male councillor said these facilities only create problems and that sometimes women are a major cause of their own troubles. He said that what some women need is "a good kick in the backside."

Not all the councillors were against the proposed transition house. Some members of council pointed out that on many occasions women need help and if there was such a facility locally, many more serious situations could be avoided. These arguments were to no avail and the Municipality of Queens became the focus of a province-wide controversy that prompted a major letter-writing campaign to council and the local media. Jane was one of many who wrote to *The Advance*. Her letter was published in the August 28 issue:

> *Dear sir:*
>
> *I just finished reading* The Advance, *dated August 14 and the following one dated August 21. I want to say that I am very appalled with the attitude of Queens Municipal Council, especially the remarks of one of the councillors.*
>
> *Unless this man has himself lived in an environment of domestic violence, I do not think that he has the right to say that "in some cases all they simply need is a kick in the backsides."*
>
> *If this man had any idea of what he was talking about he would know that once a woman takes that first kick, it is the start of an act of violence against her will. It is a terrible way to have to live—a life of suspense and fear—when you wonder at all times when the next act of violence will occur.*
>
> *Speaking from my own personal point of view, I give my full support to this, or any other transition house seeking support and assistance. For the small amount of money*

*requested by the transition house committee ($6400), I think
that the councillors who are against this should be ashamed
of themselves.*

*I do not know how many thousands of dollars my trial
cost the taxpayer, but I am sure that most of the public
support in Queens County would be in favour of this particular transition house and the small amount of funds they are
requesting as opposed to having the expense of another
costly trial, which could happen if the decision is left to such
people as represent the county at this present time.*

*It is stated in the newspaper that some councillors feel
that there are sufficient social programs currently in place
that this transition house wasn't needed. Now I ask, where
are they? and what do they offer?*

*I would like to say thank you to all those who expressed
a favourable opinion in this matter and to those who openly
supported the transition house. I pray that in the near future
these same councillors who now oppose this motion will
have a change of heart and realize just how desperately this
house is needed.*

*An ex-victim of
domestic violence
Jane (Stafford) Hurshman*

The following month, Queens Municipal Council reversed its previous decision and chose to provide its share of funding to aid in the
establishment of a transition house for the South Shore. Yet, despite all
the public outcry, three councillors still voted against the motion.
Publicly, the damage was done as Queens County became known as a
place that condones violence against women. (Years later, in 1991, a
new council refused to support an official nation-wide day of mourning
for fourteen women who were murdered in 1989 at the École
Polytechnique in Montreal.)

But pressure and lobbying does work. One of the councillors who
had vehemently opposed the motion a month earlier now said he had
given the issue a great deal of thought and was prepared to change his
decision. He said that because he had made some comments during the
last meeting without fully understanding the issue, he was prepared to

make a motion in support of the request. Furthermore, he added, he felt the county taxpayers had made it clear where they wanted their tax money spent.

Despite the three negative votes, Queens County joined with other South Shore municipal units and eventually the region's own transition house opened in Bridgewater. Today, Harbour House continues to provide a safe haven for more than one hundred-fifty battered women and their children from Lunenburg and Queens County on an annual basis.

Following the transition house controversy, Jane said she believed the original decision by Queens Municipal Council to not support the project exemplified how many people in this and other small rural communities felt about the serious issue of domestic violence. "I often wonder that if I had had access to a transition house or some other type of service whether or not I would have had to take matters into my own hands," she often said.

Of course, she reasoned, there was no way of answering that question, but she hoped other women in abusive situations would never have to face similar circumstances or make decisions like those into which she had been forced. Although she knew a transition house was not a long-term solution to such a far-reaching problem, she felt good knowing that she may have played a small part in seeing such a facility established near her home community.

Faye Jollimore, the former executive director of the South Shore Transition House which operates Harbour House, said in 1991 that a transition house can sometimes provide a "road from hell to hope" for abused women and their children. "Women and children in abusive family situations often feel trapped with no apparent way out of the serious predicament. However, there are alternatives to remaining in a situation of violence and abuse."

She added, "The sheer number of clients who have turned to Harbour House for help and shelter from an abusive family situation is an indication of the seriousness and magnitude of the problem that is domestic abuse."

While Jane realized a transition house can become the sole salvation for a woman and her children who have been trapped in abusive situations, she didn't believe these facilities were the answer. The problem is that society will not admit that domestic violence exists. "It is far too easy for wife batterers and child abusers to escape the law. The victim often becomes the focus of the law and until society begins to get tough on abusers, the rate of domestic violence will continue to grow," she said.

Judy Whitman, one of two coordinators of the Transition House Association of Nova Scotia, explains that a major attitudinal change is required before any real progress will be made in the efforts to curb domestic violence. Although it is the association's goal to act as a lobbying voice for the nine transition houses in Nova Scotia, she says the real solution to breaking the cycle of violence by getting tougher with the perpetrator.

Presently, all transition houses report being filled to capacity and, Whitman points out, that is real proof of the size of this problem. As of mid-1992, "The staff at our transition houses are working harder than they have ever worked before and there is a feeling that the demand for their services is continuing to grow at an alarming rate."

She believes that society is slowly starting to recognize the problem and with that awareness comes the needs for increased services. "But this is not happening fast enough. If we're going to recognize the problem, we must be fully prepared to do something about it and I'm not convinced that society is ready to do that yet. It's not a facility that we need, it's change of attitude."

While Whitman agrees a transition house meets a definite need, she says, "It's only a Band-Aid solution to a problem that runs very deep in society. For instance, why is it that women are the ones who have to leave their home and go to a transition house while the abusive husband gets to remain in the house with his comfortable surroundings? The husbands are the ones that are breaking the law, but yet their routine is not interrupted.

"We have to start putting more emphasis on the victims and stop making these women feel like they are to blame; we need to establish a better social support system for battered wives. And we have to start listening to women when they report their partner is abusing them. Until all these things change, transition houses will have to be the safety net for these women."

Unfortunately some women never get to that safety net and it is these women who must be reached. "There are women who never find it to the safety of a transition house and they die because the system fails."

Whitman points out that all across Canada there are examples of women who have been killed by an abusive partner, even though they had attempted to seek help from the authorities.

This scenario has been played out many times in Canada and it will continue because the system lacks the integrity to deal with the real problem: the abuser. "Statistics show us that if a man says he is going to kill his wife or girlfriend, he means it and in many cases will carry through with it." Whitman says that while this is one of the most alarming realities of domestic violence, there has been little done in Canada to address it.

That was until April 1992, when a study of spousal homicides in Nova Scotia—recommended by the Nova Scotia Advisory Council on the Status of Women—was launched by the provincial solicitor general's office. It will be the mandate of the study to examine, on a case-by-case basis, spousal homicides that occurred in Nova Scotia between 1986 and 1991. Its objectives are to determine the history of victim and offender contacts with justice, health, and social welfare agencies; to determine the nature of services and support available and provided by justice, health, and social welfare agencies; to identify risk factors associated with escalating spousal violence; and to recommend improvements in agency response, development of new programs/services to increase protection and support for victims of abuse.

The study, which initially is expected to take a year to complete, will be guided by the Spousal Homicide Study Advisory Committee which includes representatives of the Advisory Council on the Status of Women, the Transition House Association of Nova Scotia, the Department of Solicitor General and the Department of Attorney General.

Debi Forsyth-Smith is president of the Nova Scotia Advisory Council on the Status of Women, established in 1977 to monitor women's issues and act as an advisory body to the provincial government. She applauds the effort and says it is this type of affirmative action that will contribute valuable information that can be used to gain a better understanding of the domestic violence problem in the province.

Of particular value will be the information the study reveals pertaining to the history of abusive relationships that led up to the homicide. By examining actual cases, Forsyth-Smith explains the study will look at the circumstances of the relationship including the causes of the abuse and how the system may have been involved. "We want to know how long women will stay in an abusive relationship before they react and if she sought help, we want to know how she was treated."

Without a doubt, she notes, in these particular cases, something went wrong in order for the woman to kill her spouse, "and we have to know what it was. If there was a history of abuse, what type of action did these women take? Did the system fail them and why? If these women fell through the cracks in the system, then we need to know how, so that we can address the problems."

Although still in its infancy in July 1992, Forsyth-Smith indicated that interesting facts were already starting to emerge from the study. For instance, at least 35 per cent of the women who are murdered are killed by a man who, himself, has been a victim of domestic violence. "This is an interesting finding because it confirms that unless we break the cycle, domestic abuse is passed on from one generation to the next."

Early findings also showed that few women, in fact only 36 per cent, who kill their spouse may consider suicide. However, more than half of the men who kill their partner will then commit suicide. As well, research has shown that in almost all cases where a woman killed her spouse, the most common weapon was a knife whereas men tend to use a variety of weapons ranging from knives and guns to baseball bats and shoe laces. "We find that most women use a knife and there is usually only one wound, indicating the woman may have only been attempting to wound her spouse or perhaps even defend herself," says Forsyth-Smith. On the other hand, when a female is the victim, men tend to be more violent, almost as if the act of killing is one last act of torture.

Like others working closely with the issue of domestic violence, Forsyth-Smith acknowledges that one of the most common trends that appears to be emerging from the spousal homicide study is that, in most cases, abused women who killed their spouse did attempt to get help from the legal system.

"Our findings are pointing to a system that failed to protect these women," she explains, pointing out that peace bonds are one topic that continues to surface as the issue of domestic violence is examined. "Peace bonds cannot protect a woman if her spouse is intent on killing her," she adds. "Peace bonds are only effective for those men who abide by the law. That's where the system fails a victim of abuse. When a woman says she fears for her life, then she must be believed. Most women do not go to the police unless they have good reason."

While public officials and some levels of government appear now to be slowly addressing the real issues related to wife abuse and domestic violence, it was these very concerns that prevented Jane Hurshman from seeking help from the system in 1982 when she killed her abusive partner Billy Stafford.

Jane felt there was no help because she feared authorities would not believe her reports. Sadly, information presently being uncovered in the province of Nova Scotia supports her beliefs. Jane was a victim who fought back. And while her case may have been sensational, it is not unique: thousands of other women continue to live a life like the one from which Jane Hurshman escaped.

She explained that she felt she was forced into taking the law into her own hands because she saw no other way. "The police admitted that they were afraid of Bill Stafford, yet I lived with him for five years and took the beatings. If I knew these policemen were not going to deal with Bill, what was I supposed to do? Where I was supposed to go? If I went to the police, I believed I would have only ended up back with Bill and then he would have been really mad at me for going for help. He would have killed me if I had done that."

The system, Jane said, protected her tormentor and she felt her hands were tied. "It's a terrible feeling knowing that the police are afraid of the man who is pounding you around and I'm afraid there are still many women out there today who feel that way. They may be afraid of their husband, but they are also too frightened to go for help because they don't think it will do any good. If anything, they believe it will only make matters worse."

Jane hoped that change would eventually happen, but stressed that until it does there had to be a better way to help victims. "We can't allow them to continue living in isolation and pain. These women who are being tormented by their abusive partners are human beings; they are not someone's property to be banged around. These women deserve to live life with dignity, free of pain and without having to worry every day about what will happen next. Living with an abuser means living in fear every day; you're always waiting for that next shoe to drop.

"The time for action is now. As a society we are doing a very poor job helping these victims and until this changes, more and more women will continue to suffer in silence and more will continue to die."

Breaking the Silence

The hall had an air of expectation as the crowd waited to hear from the woman who had become a national hero. Women from all walks of life filled the seats and it was obvious from some of the worn, tired expressions the subject of the talk would be close to the heart. This had become a familiar setting for Jane Hurshman between 1985 and 1992 after she entered the public war on domestic violence. Often viewed as a passionate woman because of her honesty, she spoke with feeling and emotion, shedding the veil of secrecy that had protected her tormented life for more than five years.

Jane had a natural gift for making other victims feel safe. Her words could reach down from behind the podium and touch the deepest feelings of the other tormented women in the audience, regardless of the size of the crowd. Her very presence in front of the microphone commanded total attention. Her message was always clear and precise—society must bring the issue of wife abuse out in the open and put an end to the madness before more women are hurt or killed. Her words were soft but always powerful, often leaving the audience in a pool of emotions mixed with sorrow, sadness, and despair. But she always left them hope that someday the abuse would end.

First and foremost, Jane saw herself as a survivor of domestic violence. She always described herself as "one of the lucky ones" when she talked about the many years of extensive physical, sexual, and emotional abuse she had suffered at the hands of Billy Stafford. Despite the public attention Jane commanded when she spoke, she never

Photo courtesy Belle Hatfield/The Yarmouth Vanguard

By 1987, Jane Hurshman had become a vocal and highly visible opponent of domestic violence in Nova Scotia as she spoke out about wife abuse.

pretended to be something she wasn't even though many considered her to be a hero.

Publicly, Jane Hurshman was strong and vocal, but privately she was actually a shy, withdrawn person who lived behind a facade that she wanted people to see. Above all, she was a compassionate woman who longed to see society recognize wife abuse as the monster it truly is. Those who heard Jane speak about the abuse she suffered and her struggle to put her life back together agree she was a caring person who left a legacy of hope for many women in abusive relationships.

As the years went by, Jane became a strong and forceful speaker, yet her basic personality remained unchanged and she became more focused upon the kind of society that she wanted to see.

Jane envisioned a world free of wife and child abuse; a world free of violence in general. The woman who herself had been the victim of such extreme abuse felt that violence in any form could not be tolerated if people were going to have the kind of society that is fair and just. She admitted her vision of the world might be viewed by some to be hypocritical considering what she had done on the night of March 11, 1982. However, that act of violence was an act of survival. She had a choice: she could continue to live in a situation of extreme abuse where no one was doing anything to help her or she could strike back and free herself.

For Jane Hurshman, reaching the breaking point had been a long and painful journey, but in March 1982, "I felt it was either him or me." With that realization came the courage and determination to break the chains that had bound her and while she believed she had no other alternative, it was Jane's hope that other women in similar situations could find another way. It was because of that hope that in the years after her incarceration that she devoted much of her time and energy to public speaking. Inside, the effort may have been tearing her apart, but she felt compelled to help others. Bearing the burden of her own guilt for what she had done, she encouraged other victims to find a better way to end their suffering and not take the same road she had travelled.

Wendy Annand says she believes that in the years following the shooting and the sensational trials, Jane came to realize that she had been given an opportunity to extend a helping hand to others due to the bizarre circumstances in which she had lived.

"She thought of herself as a survivor and drew upon her experiences to help those still looking for a way out of their pain," she says of her friend.

In eight years, many people agree Jane Hurshman did more for the effort to fight wife abuse than government agencies and departments had done in decades. In that time, Jane became a widely recognizable figure in Nova Scotia and across Canada for her visible and outspoken, but deeply caring approach to domestic violence. Despite the personal toll this must have had on her, Jane pushed forward. It was as if she was spurred on by a belief that it was important for other battered women to know their experiences are not unique; that it was vital they knew they were not alone. Jane could have withdrawn from the public attention and into the safe sanctuary of her own personal and private world, but she felt compelled to do something.

In the years following her trial, Jane developed a very deep friendship with Rev. Margie Whynot. Before 1982, she and Jane lived close to each other in their respective South Shore communities and both had been living in abusive relationships. But while Jane's story of escape was a sensational one, Margie found a quieter way out of her situation. Following a divorce, she entered the ministry, and today she too works to help victims of domestic violence.

Margie describes her friend as a courageous and outspoken activist; a survivor. "Some will remember her as their nurse, others as a co-worker; some will remember her as their personal advocate and counsellor; and others, a strong and willing sister in our struggle to change the world. Some of us were blessed to know her as a personal friend." And in the end she stresses her great admiration for Jane.

She was a "role model—a heroine; someone for us to emulate—not for her desperate actions, but for her strengths," she says. "No one condones murder, but ten years ago we cheered her strong spirit when she took action to free herself and her children from a madman who was destroying them. And when she began to speak out in public about her experiences, she opened the door for many other victims to do the same—to break the conspiracy of silence that surrounded their lives. She became our hero—our symbol of all in our woman-spirit that is strong and brave and true."

She continues, "Jane has been a symbol of courage and hope for countless victims caught in the clutches of abusive relationships. She has been a symbol of courage and a source of inspiration for many who were working for those same victims. She has been a role model for women who have been in prison and she worked to help change the system and make their lot in life better. She was a strong feminist but, at the same time, she was different from many of the feminists I have encountered. Jane did not show any prejudice against other victims who would not or could not follow in her large footsteps; she allowed us to go on at our own pace in our own way, as long as we did something."

In an article written by Helen Branswell, which appeared in *The Chronicle-Herald* on July 31, 1986, Jane explained why she felt it was important to let other abuse victims know they are not alone. "I was totally alone and isolated and thought nobody else lived like this," she said, adding that those feelings of hopelessness mounted and grew stronger when no one came to help her, even though many people knew what was happening in the Stafford household.

Drawing from her own personal experiences, Jane wanted women to know they do not have to live in an abusive relationship despite the fact that most victims feel they have lost their independence. "When you're knocked down enough, you begin to believe that you have to live that way. Most victims just resign themselves to the fact that their life is going to be like that." But, she stressed, it does not have to be that way.

In 1986, Jane took a big step forward when she witnessed the publication of *Life With Billy*. Written by Toronto journalist and author Brian Vallée and published by Seal Books, the story opened Jane's past to anyone who wanted to explore it. Although it may have been easier for Jane to try to forget the past, she chose instead to let the world see what it was like to be a victim of domestic violence.

In an article in the *Globe and Mail* written by Deborah Jones, Jane said, following the release of the book, "I want other people in that situation to know there's other avenues available besides the route I took. That was a drastic measure.... People don't look at wife-battering as a criminal offence, it's just accepted. But it is a crime."

Wherever Jane went and regardless of whom she was addressing, her message was always the same—"Stop silently screaming behind closed doors."

In January 1987, Jane told Belle Hatfield, assistant editor of *The Yarmouth Vanguard*, that although she was legally free by that time, she would never be able to walk away from the plight of other abused women in society. "I don't want to talk about Billy anymore. I want

women to see what I've done with my life. I think I can give them hope."
And she had much to offer because she gave so freely of herself.

Jane also confided to the Yarmouth journalist that in some ways, speaking about her life after Billy was more difficult than relating the litany of horrors that occurred during her life with him. Facing life after Billy meant confrontation—with her family, with the law, with a community that had raised not one finger to help her. "But most importantly," Hatfield wrote, "she has had to confront herself."

The therapy Jane received after the shooting helped her face the past and eventually, so it seemed, she worked through her anger, hurt, and guilt. She admitted there were many times when she felt like giving up, but instead pushed forward with the help of family and friends. She tried to put her life back together and establish a normal home for herself and her children. To a degree Jane was successful, but she could never fully escape the past as her pain began to find new ways of integrating itself into her life. By 1989, the media started reporting on a new story about Jane Hurshman. Some of the headlines read: "Year probation for shoplifter" and "Hurshman fined for theft."

One account which appeared in the provincial paper, *The Chronicle-Herald*, reported Jane Hurshman was given a suspended sentence for taking a jogging suit and two plant holders worth $37.96 from a department store. Jane received one year of probation and was ordered to keep the peace.

Another article from a June 1991 issue of the same newspaper reported on another court appearance in Dartmouth. It said Jane had been charged with assault and theft of goods under $1000 — greeting cards and a bottle of cologne from a pharmacy — to which she tried to plead guilty. However, the judge ruled the assault had not been intentional and would not accept her plea to that charge. According to the newspaper report, she was fined $375.

Although Jane openly admitted to the shoplifting charges, she was devastated, fearing she had brought shame and humiliation to her family. However, she said, "I just can't help myself. It's like someone else has control over me and I don't even remember doing those things."

In the resulting court appearances on the shoplifting charges, doctors for Jane confirmed that she had been diagnosed as a kleptomaniac (a person who steals impulsively without having control of their actions). A 1989 newspaper article reported that Dr. John Curtis, a Halifax-based psychiatrist, had testified at one of Jane's shoplifting hearings where he verified that the woman suffered from kleptomania. Today, Dr. Curtis refuses to speak about his association with Jane for fear of breaching doctor-patient confidentiality.

Medical experts define kleptomania as a disorder difficult to diagnose and to treat. Symptoms of the disorder can vary from person to person, but generally an individual with kleptomania is depressed and wants to get caught. Victims of the disorder usually have no control over their actions and they disassociate themselves from their own behaviour. It is a sickness and can emerge in individuals who have experienced severe abuse such as the kind Jane suffered. These people do not steal because they want something, but because it is their way of dealing with their pain; it is a cry for help. Today, doctors across the country are diagnosing a growing number of kleptomaniacs as more and more victims of abuse are coming forward.

Dr. John Dimock, an Ottawa psychiatrist who testified at Jane's first trial in November 1982, remarks, "I had only seen Jane a few times when she was going on trial because I was mostly working with her son, Darren. I felt she was a dependent person and I am aware of the extreme pain she suffered. It is possible that the kleptomania could have been a manifestation of her past. If that's the case, it was a plea for help."

Jane had trouble dealing with this new problem and believed she was being persecuted in the media. Due to her 'celebrity' status, she made headlines each time she appeared in court and felt her shoplifting charges were an embarrassment to her family.

"It just doesn't seem fair," Jane said. "Every time I go to court for shoplifting, it seems they splash my name all over the place. Other people don't get treated that way. People go to court everyday for shoplifting and their name's not in the paper." Although she knew she would attract the media every time she was caught shoplifting, the problem continued. "I just can't seem to stop it," she added.

In addition to thinking she may have been an embarrassment to her family, Jane was also a deeply religious person and considered stealing a sin. In January 1989, she took an overdose of pills. Many speculate it was because of the shoplifting and an upcoming court appearance. Others believe it was an attempt to end the pain and guilt she continued to suffer.

According to a report on self-injuries behaviour, conducted in 1990 at the Kingston Prison for Women, female survivors of abuse often attempt to cause bodily harm to themselves, including committing suicide. Dr. Dimock says that for a woman in Jane's state of mind, even in the years following Billy's death, it would not be difficult to believe she would commit suicide. "She was strong enough to turn a gun to Billy and pull the trigger; I have no reason to think she wouldn't do something like that to herself," he says. Jane was a woman searching for help and despite her public stature and the strong image she projected, inside she was being torn apart by a variety of emotions ranging from guilt, sadness, fear, embarrassment and sorrow, to joy and happiness.

Some people, including the police, believe the shoplifting charges were sufficient motivation for Jane to commit suicide. Since 1986, she had been to court several times for shoplifting and on March 4, 1992, she was scheduled to appear in Dartmouth provincial court. This time the charges stemmed from an alleged theft from an IGA grocery store on November 16, 1991.

Jane's father, Maurice Hurshman, says he doesn't believe the shoplifting charges would cause her to take her own life. "She knew that we were not embarrassed by anything she did. We are all very proud of her and everything she did to help other people."

According to the CBC, two months before her death, Jane wrote in a letter to a friend, "I love my family very much—but I'd rather be dead than continually shame and humiliate them."

In the fall of 1991, Jane admitted her shoplifting tendencies were becoming too much to bear. She said it was like someone else had control of her body, as if she were on the outside looking in. It is a proven fact that survivors of abuse usually find an outlet for their pain and suffering. Some people may become alcoholics or anorexic, while others may suppress their feelings or find other forms of relief like compulsive gambling. Still others go to the extreme where they dissociate from reality altogether by developing multiple personality disorders or other mental ailments. And then there are those who steal compulsively; they are the kleptomaniacs. This was Jane Hurshman.

"I am getting help from my doctors to deal with the problem, but it isn't easy," sha said. "It's a constant struggle for me." In the fall of 1991, recognizing there were others with the same problem, Jane began a drive in the metro area for the creation of a support group for shoplifters.

But if this was the downside of Jane's life after Billy, then her work with victims of abuse and incarcerated women was certainly the upside. "By helping other victims, I know I am contributing something positive and giving something back to the community," Jane explained. "I feel I have something to offer these women because of my experiences and I hope to be able to give this help as long as I am able."

It was through this work that Jane was approached in 1991 by Elizabeth Forestell, executive director of the Elizabeth Fry Society, a Halifax-based organization which helps former female prisoners and women in conflict with the law. Forestell explains that because of Jane's own experiences in jail she brought an interesting and important angle to the society.

"She could see things from practical terms because she could draw from the time she spent at the Halifax Correctional Centre. Jane brought reality to our board because she could relate with the problems faced by women in prison. Because she could reflect the realities of the lives of the women we work with, she was a valuable resource. She could see things from these women's perspectives when other board members could not. In a sense, you might say she was our voice of reason."

Forestell says Jane contributed a great deal to the society in the short time she was involved. "She always managed to see the practical side of things and because of that, she kept reminding us of who we were really dealing with. Sometimes we could lose track of where we were headed because we may not have been able to relate to these women, but Jane was always there to guide us in the right direction."

Forestell says she will miss Jane's practical approach to issues as well as her energy and strength. "She had a clear vision of what kind of world she would like to see and I believe that gave her the courage to continue her work. Jane believed people have a right to live in a safe world and a right not to be abused or hurt by anyone else. With that vision she also knew there was a great deal to be done to make the kind of changes that were needed."

It was because of her work with the Elizabeth Fry Society that in the fall of 1991, Jane was appointed to the Solicitor General's Special Committee on Provincially Incarcerated Women.

In October 1991, Nova Scotia Solicitor General Joel Matheson appointed a special committee with the mandate to examine the needs of provincially incarcerated women with respect to institutional pro- gram services, nature of correctional facilities, and aftercare services.

The Solicitor General requested that the committee assess the extent to which existing programs meet the needs of the incarcerated woman and make recommendations regarding short- and long-term strategies for the provision of an optimum level of services to these women.

In forming the committee it was recognized that most women in the province's correctional system are socially disadvantaged and lack options due to unemployment, racism, and a lack of social support networks. The unique characteristics of incarcerated women in provincial correctional facilities pose distinctive problems which require creative solutions. Furthermore, it was well recognized that the existing facilities and programs were inadequate and did not meet the needs of these women. It was also recognized that the strategy for meeting the needs of this category of offender could be determined through a cooperative, consultative process involving staff of correctional services, other departments of government, community partners, and the women themselves.

In April 1992, the committee presented its report and noted that correctional administrators have struggled for many years with the unique challenges of providing appropriate programs and facilities for women sentenced to prison. "The challenge is significant primarily because of the small number of women who are incarcerated," the report stated. "One of the major stumbling blocks to establishing an appropriate program delivery structure for women prisoners has been the tendency on the part of the correctional administrators to apply concepts to women that are seen to be valid for male inmates."

One of the major findings reported by the committee was the need to develop resources in the community. "Efforts must be directed toward the development of probation hostels, residential centres, and multipurpose centres to provide correctional officials and the courts with alternatives to secure correctional facilities."

In order to carry out its mandate, the committee conducted its research between November 1991 and February 1992. One of the most disturbing realities that was uncovered was "that women's lives disappear when they go to jail. On release, they no longer have a home, a phone number, a job, or often, their children." It is true, as some point out, this also happens to male inmates, however, it was the committee's mandate to study incarcerated women.

In total, committee members interviewed thirty-three women, either previously or currently incarcerated. The interviews covered a variety of topics and included such issues as their arrest, lockup conditions, health, substance addiction, children, family, histories of abuse, conditions in the correctional centre, program needs, and suggestions for change.

Interestingly, the committee found that for many of these women the journey to jail began at home, as twenty-six of the thirty-three women interviewed reported they had been physically abused—nineteen as children or teenagers. Of the total, twenty-one reported they had been sexually abused—sixteen as children or teenagers. Additionally, twenty-seven confirmed they had experienced emotional violence. In all, thirty of the thirty-three women interviewed had been physically or sexually abused. Parents or family members were identified as the most frequent perpetrators while spouses or partners came a close second.

Although she had died before the report was released, the committee recognized the assistance Jane had provided in their efforts. As a lasting testimony to Jane's work, the committee dedicated its report to the memory of Jane Hurshman-Corkum. At the beginning of its document the committee wrote:

> *As a member of the Solicitor General's Special Committee on Provincially Incarcerated Women, she generously contributed her time and expertise to bring us understanding of the lives of incarcerated women. In many ways, she was our guide on the journey.*
> *She taught us that, while her strength and survival were remarkable, her story was not unique.*

As a result of the committee's work, it is widely believed Nova Scotia is on the brink of a new era in dealing with non-violent female offenders. The government has announced plans to phase out the Halifax Correctional Centre by 1995. Jane would have been pleased with this new direction. Only months before her death, she said, "Unless you have been in jail, you have no idea what it's like. It's almost like you are not human anymore. There needs to be change."

While Jane's work with incarcerated women brought her much personal satisfaction, she also maintained a close involvement with victims of abuse. As an unofficial volunteer counsellor and occasional crisis line worker for the Halifax-based Services for Sexual Assault

Victims, Jane would often work on a one-to-one basis with victims of abuse. It was a role she took to heart and many times, she would invite these women into her home or meet with them in the privacy of their homes where she would help by drawing upon her own life experiences. Those who worked with Jane say she never refused to help a victim in need.

Ann Keith, the executive director for the Services for Sexual Assault Victims, explains that although Jane was not a formal volunteer for their organization, she provided valuable counselling on a one-to-one basis for many women because she could identify with their pain and suffering. "We often received calls from victims wanting to talk specifically to Jane and she would willingly agree to meet with them."

Much of their association was informal, but Ann says, "Whenever I asked her how she felt about helping someone, she was always there." By agreeing to meet with these women, Jane made it possible for them to talk about their abuse, and eventually, she could guide them to finding the appropriate help. "She took on the work like it was her mission," Ann says. "She would never turn away any woman in need.

"I remember when she was getting ready for her last public appearance in December (1991) to mark the anniversary of the Montreal Massacre. When I talked to her, she told me she had been crying all week. When I asked her why, she told me she couldn't control it; thinking about the women who died there brought back all her own sad memories."

Jane did pull herself together and attended the services with approximately two hundred other citizens on December 6, 1991 to remember the fourteen women who were murdered two years earlier by Marc Lepine at L'École Polytechnique in Montreal. On that occasion, she took advantage of the chance to once again press for support for the thousands of Nova Scotian women who are being abused and suffering in silence.

An account of that event written by reporter Cathy Nicoll, which appeared in the December 7 *Daily News*, quoted Jane as saying, "Being a woman shouldn't make a difference to whether you live or die or what kind of life you lead. But, unfortunately, the headlines and the statistics show that it does."

Ann remembers Jane as a caring person who would want society to keep pushing forward with efforts to end domestic violence. "I think

Jane would want us to not give up hope and to keep on talking it out. She would not want us to go backwards after everything that has happened in recent years. She would want us to continue the struggle and she would want women, especially victims, to take care of themselves. Above all, she would not want victims to carry on alone."

She continued, "I saw some pain associated with Jane, but she would only open the door a crack, just enough to show you just a hint of what was going on with her. However, I know she wanted a world without violence."

Passiveness is the watchword of the abused woman and makes getting out very difficult. It takes courage to walk away from the threats and intimidation. Jane once said, "People ask all the time, 'How could you let that happen?' All I can say to them is unless you have been there, please don't judge—just help."

Meanwhile, Back in
Queens County

On March 10, 1991, Jane Hurshman wrote me:

*I just wanted to bring you up to date on what's happening.
On March 4, I was asked to speak out against violence
against women and the recent murders in the new year.*

*The talk and rally and march by women was held on
Saturday, March 9 at Grand Parade Square in Halifax. I
didn't like some of the reports about the recent deaths of
some of the young women as they were constantly referred
to as prostitutes. These women were people, not prostitutes.
They don't deserve to be degraded, regardless of what their
circumstances were.*

*It really bothers me that the press would pay so much
attention to that instead of dealing with the issues of violence
against women. These women were victims and sometimes
people tend to forget about that or overlook it on purpose
when they hear they may have been prostitutes. That isn't
right; they were still people.*

Early in 1991, the Province of Nova Scotia was rocked by a series
of brutal and violent crimes against women. In only a short period,
several women were killed in senseless acts that eventually led to a
province-wide call for action from the government. Rallies and vigils
were held as many citizens, both men and women, were motivated to
speak out about violence against women.

Jane was touched by these sentiments as she hoped that maybe the
people of Nova Scotia were finally getting the message about this

serious problem. However, she continued to express her dissatisfaction with the media's handling of these murders. No one, she asserted, deserved to be treated with anything less than respect and dignity — regardless of the direction their lives may have taken.

In a conversation following this rally, Jane said she was outraged at how the media and some facets of society had responded to the latest wave of violent crimes against women. "I really am appalled and disgusted by what we've seen. It's almost because some of these women were labelled as prostitutes that people don't care what's happened to them. But they forget these women were human beings and if they were prostitutes then maybe they had good reason and maybe they had no other choice.

"Even after all that's been done in recent years, many people still do not accept that violence against women is a real problem. Everyday, I hear people say, 'she deserved it' or 'she got what she wanted' or 'she asked for it.' I don't understand how people could believe those kinds of things. And it isn't only men who think that way; there are many women who also believe this kind of reasoning as well."

But, she added, "These people aren't living in the real world. How can they honestly believe that a woman could ask to be knocked around and walked over all the time? I fail to understand how anyone could think that a woman will stay in a violent relationship because she likes it. If she stays, it is usually because she feels trapped, or because she doesn't know how to get out." Despite all the studies that have been done and all the task forces that have been formed, "I think we're just going through the motions, trying to make it look like we're doing something. But until we actually see some tangible action to deal with the abuser, no amount of study will change anything."

It was also during this conversation that Jane talked about an upcoming project that would see her life story told in a movie for CBC television. In the spring of 1991, it was confirmed plans were being finalized for the movie. While she admitted to being overwhelmed by the prospect, she had agreed to the project because she felt it was another way to help victims of abuse.

The movie is to be based on the book *Life With Billy*. The author, Brian Vallée, in support of the movie said, "This is a very important story about a serious subject that must be told." Because Jane's story was so poignant, Vallée believes the movie can bring more of the public's attention to the issue of wife battering.

For that reason, Jane agreed to the movie, although she acknowledged that the project would result in further publicity. Her greatest fear was that the story could be sensationalized. Despite the headline-grabbing details of her life, she did not want the story to be exploited. "I believe it will be very beneficial to tell this story in a movie because of the public awareness it will create. Even though the book has been out for many years, I still think there are people like me who haven't read it and who still don't know where to find help. I think the movie will get to some of these people because everyone watches TV and if it helps them, then that's great.

"Even though so much time has passed since I did what I did, the message is still important—that women are being abused."

She believed the movie and other projects to which she had agreed would be important vehicles through which the issue of wife abuse could be explored. "I would never agree to do these types of things, if I felt they would be sensationalized. I want the movie to be honest and helpful for those who may not know where to turn."

While she knew some people would be critical of the movie project, "or anything I do for that matter," Jane said she believed issues such as domestic violence need attention. "I've met many people who have told me they found help after reading the book. To me, that's what's important; I only wish I had had some help back then, but ten years ago the media was not paying much attention to these problems."

It came as no surprise that when *The Advance* published the news of the movie project we were inundated with public opinion. Many local citizens still harbour restentment towards Jane and feel far too much attention has been paid her.

Margaret Joudrey, the woman whom Jane had thought of as a second mother while she lived in Bangs Falls, is one of those Queens County residents who does not believe the stories related by Jane, and she is quick to take every opportunity to express her views. A resident of Bangs Falls for more than forty years, Margaret willingly tells how she feels about Jane Hurshman and the events that surround the night of March 11, 1982. "No one knows the truth about what supposedly went on in Billy and Jane's house. All they hear is Jane's side of the story," most of which she points out "is a pack of lies."

Today, Margaret continues to live in the small trailer which Jane says Billy had threatened to burn down. She lives alone now and in a conversation in the spring of 1992, the small-featured woman recalled those years before Billy was shot. She is adamant in her disbelief of the events as described by Jane. As she speaks, she forcefully emphasizes that, in her opinion, the abuse that Jane was supposed to have taken from Billy between 1977 and 1982 "just didn't happen."

Margaret says she has vivid memories of the events that transpired on that night. Her eyes narrow as she says she can also remember the years before that date, "and I never ever saw Billy lay a hand on Jane."

Billy had met Stan Joudrey, Margaret's husband, in the mid-1970s while they were both working in the woods for a local forester. "It was Stan who offered Billy the land behind our trailer when they needed a place to put their house." After Billy and Jane moved to Bangs Falls in 1977, a close friendship developed between the two women. It was a bond that lasted until the night Jane shot Billy Stafford.

"Jane was like a daughter to me in those days," Margaret recalls and says that while some people think "I turned against Jane because she got me involved in so much trouble by pulling me into court, that isn't the case. I liked Jane and I liked Billy but it bothers me that she got away with murder. That's what I'm so upset about."

Margaret speaks with conviction when she says in her opinion Jane's stories and allegations of abuse are false. "They're all made up by her. I never saw anything between them and I lived close to them for five years. I never, ever once saw Bill lay a hand on Jane. But I think she made up all that stuff because it was beat into her head that if she claimed he hit her, she could get off. And it worked."

Referring to notes that she claims to have seen in Jane's possession following the second trial and acknowledging that Jane had developed a large following of believers who saw her as their hero, Margaret continues, "I don't believe a single word she said. She made a lot of that stuff up for the book." Margaret says she's sure some of the information is false, but readily admits she has never actually read *Life With Billy* and doesn't know what the book contains. "I knew what she was going to write about and I wouldn't read it because none of it's true; I don't believe any of it." As a matter of fact, she adds, "I won't let that damn book in my house. I don't want that garbage in here."

Jane's book caused such a sensation when it was first published that Margaret says she warned visitors to her home not to mention it. "I didn't want to hear about the lies she wrote. I don't know how people can believe all that and talk about it like they know it happened, when they weren't here. All they're doing is taking Jane's word for it and I say it ain't true. I never saw her have any bruises and I never heard Bill fire any guns at her."

In Margaret's opinion, Billy was painted as an evil person during the trial, but she says, "Billy was a good person." It is Jane whom she describes as the "bad one."

"I'm not taking up for Bill because he could get mad just like everyone else, but he wasn't as bad as Jane said he was," Margaret claims. In fact, contrary to what some people said on the witness stand at Jane's trial, she says she liked Billy Stafford. "He told me and Stan that we were the only friends he had and he treated us good. If he bought his mother a plant or flowers, he bought the same for me; he said he looked at me as his mother away from home."

After Stan died in 1979, Margaret says her friendship with Billy and Jane grew even stronger. "We were good friends. I saw many things happen in that house, but it wasn't done by Bill. I kind of thought of him as some kind of overgrown kid." Only days before Billy died, Margaret recalls a conversation she had with him. "He had asked me if I had anything I wanted done and then right out of the blue he said 'I love you more than my own mother.' That don't sound like a bad person to me."

Despite the strong friendship Margaret and Jane shared, she says everything changed after the night of March 11, 1982. Her complexion turns red and her voice grows brisk when she states, "She killed him and I didn't like that. She just went kind of berserk throwing out pictures and stuff. It was like she was anxious to get rid of everything; like she was trying to forget he was ever around. If you ask me, I would say the wrong one went that night."

Abuse, if it happened, would be a terrible thing, Margaret agrees, but quickly points out that in her opinion, "It didn't happen in their house because Bill never hit her. All these people know is what Jane tells them, but what about Bill's story? Who's going to tell that? He was all mouth, that I agree, but he was kind-hearted and wouldn't hurt nobody."

Billy Stafford was forty-one years old when he died and Margaret describes his death as a crime. "She murdered him and got away with it. She wasn't a hero to me. She was a murderer and that stuff she made up is just garbage."

Jane agrees herself that she should have gone to jail for a long time after admitting to killing Billy. "That would have made a lot of people around here feel a whole lot better. Instead, they let her go free," Margaret says. In the years after Jane moved from Bangs Falls, Margaret says she visited a few times, "But she never talked about it at all. In fact, she never mentioned Bill's name at all. I never turned her away when she came to visit; I didn't get down and hate her."

Margaret says despite the stories she hears about Billy Stafford, she will never believe that he abused Jane or the children. Shaking her head she continues with conviction, "I just couldn't stand all her lies. I don't believe that Bill was going to burn my trailer that night because he wouldn't hurt me. If anything, he'd give you the shirt right off his back; he was that kind of a guy."

Even ten years after his death, Margaret says she still mourns Billy for what happened that night. Motioning toward the small, yellow house situated only a few hundred feet further up the driveway that once belonged to Billy and Jane Stafford, she adds, "I still pity him for what happened. If he was doing all that stuff to her, why didn't she leave? She didn't have to kill him. If he was the way she described him, then I would say maybe he deserved what he got, but I don't believe he was. However, all we are supposed to go by is what she said."

A river of emotions runs deep in Margaret Joudrey as she adamantly discredits the allegations of abuse that Jane says she suffers. "Those were hard times after she killed Bill." She believes that in the months following Billy's death she saw his ghost. "In the day time, when I looked up at the house, I swear I could see him standing there in his short-sleeved white shirt. I just got the feeling that he wanted to tell me something."

Following Jane's death in February 1992, Margaret coldly admits she had no remorse for the woman. "When it came over the radio that she was dead, I said 'good.' I didn't feel sorry for her because I don't believe what she did was right. Maybe she paid for it in the end."

While some callers to *The Advance* office and Margaret Joudrey were vocal about their animosity toward Jane Hurshman, others tend to be more tactful. However, the bottom line is that many resent the visibility and reputation that Jane had gained. As the rest of the province applauded her efforts, back in Queens County, it was a whole different story.

The World
According to Jane

Perhaps it was an omen or merely a coincidence that I had made arrangements to meet with Jane Hurshman on Friday, September 13, 1991, to discuss an article we had been planning for a number of months. Earlier in the year, she had agreed to give an interview, the basis of which would be used to produce an in-depth article that would be published the following March to mark the tenth anniversary of the night she shot Billy Stafford.

We had spoken a number of times on the phone since March and finally we were ready for the interview. I had cleared my entire afternoon to ensure we would have sufficient time to cover as many topics as she thought appropriate. The concept behind the article was not only to provide an update about what life had been like for Jane Hurshman in the ten years following the shooting and resulting trials, but also to show people that an abuse survivor can make a new beginning through perseverance and determination. Jane made it clear that the only reason she would agree to an article was to spread her message that the silence must be broken.

The meeting was set for 1 p.m. We chose Wong's Restaurant, one of the local favourites. A comfortable Chinese eatery in downtown Liverpool, Wong's would not only be a good place for lunch, but it would also provide a safe, neutral setting where Jane might feel more at ease. She was somewhat hesitant about spending time in the Town of Liverpool because of all the painful memories, so I suggested a location where her presence might not attract so much attention.

Jane felt comfortable about meeting at Wong's and so we began. I didn't know it then, but I was setting the stage for what would be Jane's last public interview; five months later she would be dead.

The weather was nice on that late summer afternoon. I remember thinking how fortunate we were not to have had any rain or fog that day. The restaurant was full, as it is almost every Friday. Many of the locals like to dine out for lunch at the end of the week, and many choose Wong's because the food and service is good.

Looking around the packed dining room, I spotted a friendly face in the crowd looking in my direction. At that instant, I had the feeling that she was either beginning to wonder if I was going to show or she was thinking about leaving. I knew I was on time, but I hoped she had not had second thoughts about the interview. Quickly, I made my way to the table, hoping to put her more at ease. Sitting down, I asked if she was alright.

"I'm fine," she assured me. Looking at her watch, she pointed out she had arrived ten minutes early and was getting a little hungry sitting there watching the other customers being served. Feeling relieved, I suggested that we would eat here and then go back to my home for the interview where we could talk privately. She agreed.

As we scanned the menu, making small talk, I asked if she felt uncomfortable about coming back home.

"Sometimes I do," she responded. "I spend a lot of time at my Mom's and Dad's in Danesville, but I don't come into town very much." She suggested that perhaps she was being paranoid, but whenever she was in Liverpool she had the feeling that people were staring at her and that made her uneasy. "I realize that there's still a lot of bad feelings in Liverpool about what happened even if it was ten years ago," she explained, bowing her head almost as if in shame.

I reassured her that while there may be some people in this community who resented what had taken place a decade ago, there were others who understood her situation. My reassurance seemed to do little good.

"I could never come back here to live," Jane argued. "There are some people who would never forget or forgive me. Besides, there are just too many bad memories here." I suggested that we should forget about the rest of Queens County and concentrate on her. I told her I wanted to know what was happening with her.

"What was life like after Billy?" I asked, ignorant to the fact that I had just crossed a boundary.

"Please don't refer to this as 'life after Billy'," she shot back. "I'm so tired of hearing that phrase. It's almost like I don't have a life of my own or my own identity. Whenever people talk about me or the media does anything on my work, they always refer to me as having a life after Billy. I do have my own life and Bill hasn't been a part of it for ten years. I wish people would refer to me as Jane Hurshman and forget about tacking on that phrase."

Although I was somewhat taken aback by Jane's sudden and vehement stance, I quickly assured her that I would not use 'that' phrase anymore and that I would not use it for the title of my article. How ironic her request was to become in less than six months. It was almost prophetic—could she have known then that her life, still in the shadow of Billy Stafford, would soon be cut short.

Reassured, Jane dug deep into her dark-coloured handbag. Pulling out some folded papers that distinctively looked like an invitation, she extended it in my direction. "This is for you and Nancy [my wife]," she said. I carefully scanned the invitation. It read:

This is the day the Lord hath made—
A day of happy beginnings
when we:
Jane Marie Hurshman and
Joel Stephen Corkum
pledge our love as one
on Thursday, October tenth
nineteen hundred and ninety one
at two o'clock in the afternoon
St. John's Evangelical Lutheran Church
Mahone Bay, Nova Scotia
Rev. P. George Wawin officiating
Our joy will be more complete
if you can join in our celebration of love

The look on my face must have been one of bewilderment because she joked, "Don't be so surprised. I'm really happy about this. He's a wonderful guy and it's going to be a whole new beginning for me."

Instead of asking her about her fiancée as I should have done, I inquired about her choice of locations for the wedding.

"It's neutral ground," she answered, then paused for a few minutes, collecting her thoughts. "There's still a lot of Bill's family around here so I didn't think it would be right for me to get married in Queens County. And I didn't want the wedding in Halifax because of the press." As a matter of fact, she pointed out, I would be the only media person she was inviting. "I would like you to be there just as a friend, but I trust you and if you want to use anything from the wedding in your article, you can. I just don't want the wedding to be a big media event, that's all."

By this time, curiosity had gotten the best of me and I pushed for details about Joel Corkum. Her answers were honest and from the heart. She beamed with enthusiasm as she talked about him and I could tell she had found someone who obviously made her happy.

"I met Joel about a year-and-a-half ago in Bridgewater through a mutual friend," she confided. He was a mechanic from Lunenburg County. "He's such a wonderful man and he's helping me to forget all about the bad things that happened all those years ago." She explained that after all the years of pain and suffering, she had finally found someone who made her happy and, she felt, truly loved her.

"I've had so much pain in my life that it's hard to believe that I could find someone who is so loving and caring and thoughtful," Jane continued, with emotion. "He's really good to me and makes me feel like a human being." Jane admitted, however, that she had been reluctant at first to get involved in another relationship.

"I was really scared at first. For all those years after the trial, I didn't know if I wanted to get involved in another relationship but after I met Joel, all of that changed." Her commitment to this man was strong. "I really love Joel because he takes me as I am. He knows my past and it doesn't seem to bother him. He doesn't push me for details but lets me talk about it on my own. And that's good because there's no pressure. I don't have to try to explain things to him and that's what makes him so special. He really understands what I've gone through and gives me the space I need."

From Jane's description of their relationship, it was obvious that she was prepared to make a life-long commitment to Joel. "He takes me for who I am, and that's really all I can expect. I can't ask for anything more."

I inquired how the children got along with Joel.

"Everyone likes him very much, including my family and my sons," she replied. "They all get along very well and that's good because it makes everything so much easier. I think that after all these years, I will finally have a chance for a normal life. After I get married, I'm going to try to put as much space between me and my past as possible and I know Joel will be there to help."

As for her children, Jane had mixed feelings about how they were coping with life and about their future. "My sons are doing alright. Allen is married to a lovely girl from Cape Breton and they both work and have a nice home in Dartmouth. Jamie graduated from high school last year and is working. As for Darren, well, my baby is fourteen years old now. He is still having some problems and he is having some extensive therapy now which he started earlier this year."

Although Darren was still having difficulty dealing with his past, Jane was hopeful he would be alright. "He has a really good doctor. Dr. (John) Curtis has worked with both Darren and me and he feels Darren is making progress. He just needs to know that I love him very much, as I do all my boys."

On that note, the conversation ended. Other than casual comments, Jane remained silent while we ate. It was obvious to me that there was still an inner torment behind her positive facade and this mask only thinly disguised it. It seemed to me that Darren's struggles to gain a normal childhood distressed her and her love for him tore her apart in the face of his difficulties. Cautiously, I asked if that was the case.

She responded hesitantly. "I don't know, it's just that sometimes, everything that happened in the past seems to just sneak up on me all at once. Maybe it's because I'm back here where it all happened. Or sometimes it happens when I'm talking about the kids and the past." She paused, as though withdrawing. "But I'll be alright. We'll be able to talk." I decided not to ask any more questions at that point. We finished our lunch and left the restaurant in silence.

As Jane enjoyed driving, we took her car. "I feel like I'm the one in control when I drive," she said. I assured her I had no problem with that but jokingly suggested that I be the navigator. I chose a route that took us past the Liverpool courthouse.

As we passed the historic structure, she slowed down, almost as if she was looking for something or someone. Then she asked, "Do you mind if we stop here for a second?" I didn't mind. In fact, I selfishly thought stopping might be a good way to get our interview back on track. I asked if there was anything in particular she wanted to look at.

"No," she shot back. "I just want to have a look around." Parking the car in front of the courthouse, she got out and cautiously walked up the wooden steps that lead up to the black doors. "You know, being here brings back all the memories; it's almost as if everything happened only yesterday," Jane began as she passed her hand over the painted doors. "Sometimes, it all seems like it was a bad dream; like a nightmare. But being here today by this courthouse makes it all seem so real. I remember everything: how I felt the day I took the stand, how I felt when the reporters crowded around me for comments, how it felt that day when the jury found me not guilty, and how I felt the second time I came back to court. It was on that day that I felt everything was finally over, at least as far as the courts were concerned."

That was the second time that Jane had made a conditional statement since our conversation began before lunch. I knew there was more going on in her mind than she was telling me. Selecting my words carefully, I asked how she was coping with her past and with life in general.

"Things are good. I don't think much about the past anymore, but every now and then, I think of Bill," she answered, while bending to sweep off a section of one of the steps. Sitting down, she leaned her head against one of the large white pillars that adorn the front of the courthouse and closed her eyes. "Sometimes I just can't seem to get him out of my head; he was a sociopath, you know. Bill had no conscience; nothing seemed to bother him. I don't know how anybody could be like that. I've spent a lot of time in the past ten years thinking about what he did and wondering how he could have done all that without having any feelings for me or the kids. He hurt us real bad, you know."

Then there was silence. She bolted up straight and as she stared at the step beneath her feet, without prompting, began asking me some pointed questions.

"Do you believe that Billy did all those things?"

It seemed strange that after all these years she would ask me whether I believed the allegations of abuse.

"I know there are cruel people out there in the world who do a lot of bad things to people they are supposed to love," I said. I believe Billy was one of those people.

"But do you believe that Bill really would have killed me?"

I had not personally known Billy Stafford but I had spoken with a number of impartial people about him in the years following her trials and these people assured me that, indeed, Billy Stafford was more than capable of carrying through on his threats. Based on that information, I told her I believed that Billy seemed to be the type of man who could hurt anyone. But, I assured her, he could not hurt her anymore.

"Sometimes I wonder what would have happened if I hadn't done that ten years ago," she said without emotion.

More silence, then she caught me off guard by asking a question that had no bearing on the subject. "Do you ever think of Jock Inglis?"

I was speechless. Jock Inglis was the editor of *The Advance* who assigned me to cover her trial in the fall of 1982. Jock was a very close friend who died suddenly in December 1986. Jock had been a special person and I considered him my mentor. His death had been hard to accept. I thought of him as friend and Jane knew how I felt because we had talked about that shortly after his death.

"Why do you want to know?" I asked. It didn't cross my mind at the time, but later I realized this is the type of question you might expect to get from someone considering suicide.

She answered quickly, almost as if she was expecting the question. "Just curious. When someone close to you dies, it leaves an impact on the rest of your life. I just wondered how you were doing."

I felt uneasy about her questions. What could Jock's death five years ago have to do with our conversation, I wondered. Was this a cry for help?

"I saved the clippings from when he died," she continued, attempting to explain the rationale behind her questions. "He seemed like a nice guy; he wrote some really good things about my trial. It was sad the way he died all of a sudden without any warning. That must have been hard on all of you, but sometimes life gets too hard to continue. I guess if you don't know what's going on in someone's mind, you can't expect to know why they'd do something like that."

She sprang to her feet and headed toward her car. "I'm ready to go now."

Hesitantly, I followed, but I couldn't shake my sense of unease. Within minutes of leaving the courthouse, we were at my home and as we entered the living room, Jane's attention was taken by an eight-by-ten-inch portrait of my infant son on a table. He had been born earlier that year on February 14.

"He looks like a lovely baby," she remarked, picking up the framed picture and pressing her fingers to the glass. Then, placing the photo back in its position, she slumped in a big armchair near the table. "It's too bad all children can't grow up in a home where they're loved and wanted. Some children only know pain and suffering. It just doesn't seem right that there are parents out there who abuse their children. Don't they know they're ruining those kids' futures? Those kids will never have a chance at a normal life."

Again, it was easy to see inside this woman. Obviously she understood the pain and suffering of abused children and, at that particular moment, of her own young child, Darren.

I tried to lift her out of her mood by pointing out that ten years ago, Jane Stafford had become a household name in Canada as the woman who struck back at her tormentor. She seemed immediately overwhelmed by such a summation.

"That's not really who I am," she interrupted. "I'm just Jane Hurshman, a woman who survived years of abuse and now wants to help other women."

Patiently I explained the world saw Jane Hurshman as a survivor, and that Jane Stafford, the abuse victim, no longer existed.

She nodded in agreement, but added that she was only able to accept that description because of extensive therapy and the love and support of her family and friends. "It hasn't been an easy ten years, but I now feel I can put things in order. For the most part, I've been able to put Billy Stafford and those years of suffering away on a shelf where they can no longer hurt me, although they do come back to haunt me on a regular basis."

During the years that followed the shooting and the resulting trials, Jane pointed out she had worked hard to put her life back together. "I wanted my life to have some sort of meaning," she said, alluding to the fact that she had been working as a certified nursing assistant at the Halifax County Regional Rehabilitation Centre in Dartmouth. "I enjoy my job because it allows me to help people," she added, pointing out that her responsibilities were mainly to work with emotionally and mentally ill patients.

"When I first moved to the city [Halifax], I didn't know a soul, but I knew the things I wanted to do the most—make a good home for my kids, get a good job, and help other women so they didn't end up like me."

Although in the immediate years following her ordeal, Jane had been called upon regularly to speak at functions about domestic abuse and had felt compelled to do her part, she explained, "I don't do a lot of public speaking anymore these days. It's been so many years that I don't have the emotion anymore that you need when you're in front of a large group." But she knew the public pressure would not go away and that while her schedule of appearances might have diminished, her story and its message was still important. Could it be, I wondered, that Jane was using her public work to avoid her own inner horrors. I realized how visibly tired she really was. Here was a woman who was getting married in a month's time, insisted she had a great deal to live for, and yet seemed so emotionally exhausted, that she was almost on the verge of collapse.

She rested her head against the chair back and closed her eyes. The conversation became mechanical and I was aware that Jane was reciting a rehearsed response to my questions in an attempt to give me the answers that she thought I wanted to hear. Reluctantly, I concluded that she didn't want to do this interview after all. Although I had hoped to find a new perspective on the Jane Hurshman story, I understood she was only showing me the woman that she wanted the world to see.

"I believe it is very beneficial to tell my story because of the public awareness it creates," she continued in a monotonous tone, her arms tightly folded around her chest. "I still know there are people in trouble who don't know where to find help."

She got up from the chair and again picked up the photograph of my son before continuing. "Even though so much time has passed, the message is still important—that women are being abused. I hope my story will get to some of these people and show them that they can find a way to get out."

As to the attention she would receive because of the upcoming movie, Jane just shrugged her shoulders. She put the picture back and sat down. "It will be hard to see the movie come to life because of all the memories it will bring back. I'm not the same person now that I was back then. It's almost like that wasn't really me, but the movie will bring it all back. I know that."

While she agreed there will be some who may be critical of the movie project because they see it as being exploitative, Jane believed issues such as domestic abuse need as much media attention as possible. "I will admit things are a lot different today than they were ten years ago because of all the public attention and educational programs, but there's a long way to go in really addressing this problem. I only wish I had some help back then, but ten years ago, I couldn't find it."

Over the past decade, she pointed out, some people had misunderstood her motives. "But you can never get through to these people because they won't admit that wife abuse happens. You don't become an abused woman just to become famous or to write a book."

She sighed, "That's a high price to pay for fame."

Jane insisted she did not like being considered a celebrity. "That's a hard thing to live up to. It doesn't give you any room to be human; it doesn't give you chance to fall down once in a while. It's really not fair that people put you on a pedestal. Sometimes I feel like I'm under a microscope. But," she paused to gather her thoughts, "you learn to cope with the attention and live with it."

On the surface, Jane accepted the fact that being the centre of a sensational trial, as well as the subject of a book and movie, brought with it a certain level of celebrity status. "I didn't ask for it, but I got it so I have to learn to deal with it accordingly and keep things in perspective."

However, keeping that perspective isn't always easy, she admitted.

Jane openly acknowledged that there are many things in her past she would change if she could, but forcefully insisted that striking back at the abusive Billy Stafford was not one of them. "I still have regrets that I got myself involved with him in the first place. But I am not sorry that Bill is dead. I've accepted the fact a long time ago that if he wasn't dead, then I would have been. I know I would have never gotten away from him if he was still alive."

Her voice turned softer and she began to relax as she admitted she was remorseful, even if it wasn't for Billy Stafford. "I feel sorry for all those other women who are living the life I suffered. And I feel for those men who can't help themselves because that's where the system fails. There is no help for the violator either. I knew what I was doing when I picked up that gun but I was prepared to go to jail if it meant I could get away from him. I figured I was already doing time with him and there was no other way out."

Jane said in her opinion it is the system that is partly to blame for the way things are. She suggested that when abusers come to court, it should be mandatory that they seek counselling for their problem. "These men are not all Billy Staffords; some of them really want help." But until society makes a more concentrated effort to help abusers break the cycle of violence, "I don't think the problems of wife abuse or domestic violence will ever go away."

Although Jane kept insisting she was getting her life back together, she revealed, "It's a constant struggle every day just to keep my life in a straight path and I know it will be a struggle for the rest of my life."

She readily confessed to being a compulsive shoplifter. "But it isn't because I need these things. It's my way of dealing with the past. I just can't control it. I'm getting help from my doctors to deal with the problem, but it isn't easy. It's a constant struggle for me." She proudly noted that at that time she was spearheading a drive in the metro area for the creation of a support group for shoplifters.

She paused, gazing blankly out the window. "When I talk to women who are being abused, I tell them to never stop fighting back. I encourage them to let people know what kind of life they're living. Victims have to go after help and they can't keep this sort of thing a secret. Silence is an abuse victim's worst enemy."

Seeing her emotional exhaustion, I suggested we take a break and I would take some pictures of her. After a brief photo session on the back deck, I told her that unless there was something else she wanted to say we could call it quits. On our way back to the car, she pointed out how fresh the air always seemed to be in Queens County.

"That's one of the things I always liked about living next to the ocean," she reflected. "But sometimes when you're trapped in your own little world, your private hell, you don't notice or appreciate those little things and that's too bad."

We said goodbye. I would see her again in a month's time at the wedding when Jane and Joel would exchange their vows in an intimate ceremony, witnessed only by members of the family and close friends.

On October 10, a small group of well-wishers congregated at St. John's Evangelical Lutheran Church in Mahone Bay to witness the union of Jane Hurshman and Joel Corkum. Jane had been a lovely bride. Dressed in blue, she proudly walked down the aisle on her father's arm. Truly, this was a blessed day for the woman who had for so long struggled to have a normal life and a loving relationship. She beamed with happiness as she met Joel at the altar to exchange vows.

"This is the happiest day of my life," she said to the small group of family and friends gathered to share her joy. Five months later, however,

On October 10, 1991, family members and close friends gathered at St. John's Evangelical Lutheran Church in Mahone Bay to witness the wedding of Jane Hurshman and Joel Corkum.

that joy would turn to sorrow as the small group would gather again at the same church to mourn Jane's death.

Returning to my office later the afternoon of our interview, I reflected on the previous couple of hours. I realized that though Jane no longer lived under Billy Stafford's tyranny, he still had control over her. Even after ten years, the emotional baggage remained. I remember thinking what a tragedy her life was.

But that life was to end on the weekend of February 21, 1992. At that point, the article based on our conversation had been written and was scheduled to be published on Wednesday, March 11, exactly ten years to the day after the now-famous shooting. However, on Monday morning, February 24, Halifax police confirmed that her body had been found in a parked car a day earlier. Initially, we had thought about shelving the article out of respect for Jane and because we did not want to be seen as exploiting her death. Instead, however, we came to believe that Jane would have wanted her story told because of the issues in which she so vehemently believed and the causes to which she had devoted her life. After all, she had broken the silence.

Jane and Joel Corkum with her parents, Gladys and Maurice Hurshman, outside the church after Jane's wedding ceremony.

Mrs Jane Hurshman-Corkum with her new husband Joel and two of her sons, Darren (far left) and Jamie Whynot (far right), during the wedding celebrations in Mahone Bay, a picturesque seaside community halfway between Halifax and Queen's County.

An Angel With
Dirty Fingernails

Saturday, February 22, 1992, was a cold winter night. The North Atlantic winds blew along the frozen coastline of Nova Scotia and it had been snowing almost the entire weekend. Although spring was only a month away, it has long been accepted by Maritimers that the last part of February can be the most dreary and harshest part of the winter. The best place to be on a night like that was at home. And that's where most people were, except for the Halifax police. The had begun a frantic search for a missing woman.

Although police in the metro area had been searching for Jane since around 1 a.m. that Saturday, news of her disappearance had not yet made its way to Liverpool. Jane's family and friends had no idea of what was happening only a few hundred kilometres away. Nor did they know about the bizarre, yet tragic, story that was about to unfold.

It was about eleven o'clock when the RCMP officer called me from the Cole Harbour RCMP detachment. During my ten years as a journalist I had spoken with the police on countless occasions, but I had never before been called by an RCMP officer at my home at such a late hour. At first, I thought it was a prank call, but I quickly realized that this was for real.

"We're investigating the disappearance of Mrs. Jane Hurshman-Corkum," he stated matter-of-factly. "We found your phone number in some of her papers and we were wondering if she may have contacted you in the past day or so."

Naturally, I was astonished. I told the officer that I had not spoken with Jane for four days, since the preceding Wednesday. He asked if I would contact the detachment in Liverpool if I heard from Jane, and hung up.

There was no time for questions or for explanations. I spent the rest of the night thinking about the constable's call and about what he had said: Jane was missing!

Laying in bed, half dreading and half wanting the phone to ring a second time, I recalled the conversation we had had only a few days earlier. On Wednesday, February 19, I had phoned Jane to review some of the material that I wanted to use in the article. Now, here I was, four days later, wondering if she were dead or alive. In light of the phone call I had just received from the Cole Harbour RCMP, I knew there was reason for concern, but I had no idea how serious the situation was.

Once news of Jane's disappearance finally reached Queens County, it didn't take long for the stories and rumours to spread. By lunchtime on Sunday, February 23, the popular speculation circulating throughout the community was that someone had taken Jane somewhere and killed her. Surely, I hoped, they must be wrong. There must be some reasonable explanation for her disappearance.

As afternoon turned into evening, the supper time news broadcast pictures of a blue car discovered at the Halifax waterfront parking lot. It was believed to be Jane's. These reports also indicated that her dead body had been found in the vehicle, the apparent victim of a single gunshot wound. Later that evening, a member of Jane's family phoned to confirm the sad news. Although the police were not releasing details, they confirmed that, indeed, it was Jane's body they had found in the car.

The week passed quickly as newspapers and television newscasts carried conflicting stories about Jane's untimely death. There was much speculation on the part of the media and the authorities, but there were few specific facts. It was only a matter of days before the suicide theory began circulating. Authorities were quick to point out that although they had not yet ruled out foul play, they suspected Jane had taken her own life and had made it look like murder. Either way, she was dead.

On February 28, about one hundred family members and close friends gathered at St. John's Evangelical Lutheran Church in Mahone Bay, the same church Jane and Joel had been married in. It was a somber farewell as the group mourned the loss of a caring family member and a close, warm friend. But it was also an inspirational service led by Rev. P. George Wawin as those who had known Jane shared their fond memories of the woman who had died so tragically.

At the front of the church, near the altar, a small table was stationed beneath a solitary, hanging candle and on that table sat a picture of Jane and an urn that contained her remains. The absence of her body made the service seem more like a dream than a reality. However, watching the relatives and friends pile into the church, I knew this was, indeed, actually happening.

Thinking back to the previous fall, I remembered a conversation Jane and I had shared. During that conversation I discovered that Jane had learned to accept death as being part of life. Two years earlier, my only sister, Heather, had been diagnosed with leukemia. It was a difficult two years and on September 16, 1991, she succumbed to the ravages of the disease. A few days after we had buried my sister, Jane called while I was at work, to see how I was doing. Now, five months later, while sitting at her own funeral, it seemed fitting that her words of comfort and concern rushed back.

"Dying is part of living," she had told me. "I know it is painful to lose someone you love or someone you're close to, but we're all going to have to face it sooner or later. I believe that people are put here for a specific purpose and a specific amount of time. When you've done what you're supposed to do and your time is up, then it's time for you to go."

Pointing out that my sister had left behind two young children, it was Jane's advice to remember the good things about her life, even if it was short, and to help her children remember those things about their mother. "Don't dwell on the things that were bad or about the fact that she is gone. Remember what made her happy and what she did to make others happy. These are the things that she has left behind."

I was now giving myself the same advice. Although Heather was only thirty-two years old when she died, Jane had believed her death was God's wish. "Don't ask yourself questions that you're not going to find answers to," she cautioned. "I'm not saying that you shouldn't mourn her death, but you can't let yourself dwell on the unknown. There are people younger than your sister who die every day. You must be thankful for the time that she had and go forward."

Perhaps her words were only common sense, but at that time in my life they were comforting. Instinctively, Jane seemed to know when others were in need of a kind word and was always there to provide it. I had come to realize that Jane put the feelings of others above her own and now, many of those whom she had touched in one way or another were there to say thanks in their own private way.

Glancing around the church, I could see familiar faces of family and friends from Queens County as well as strangers whom I had never seen before. These must have been some of Jane's work colleagues and abuse victims whom she helped at some point. I was right on both counts.

The service began with prayers and hymns. The church overflowed with emotion, but many seemed to be trying to hold back the tears in an effort to keep a brave face. Jane, too, had always attempted to maintain a strong facade but in the end that public image may have become too much to bear.

Perhaps it was Rev. Margie Whynot who had come to understand

Photo courtesy Nadine Fownes/The Chronicle-Herald

On Friday, February 28, about 100 family members and friends gathered to say their final farewell to Jane Hurshman-Corkum at the same church in Mahone Bay where Jane and Joel Corkum had only months earlier been married.

that truth better than most. She had come to know Jane better than anyone else in the years following the death of Billy Stafford and on this day she was giving the eulogy, which she affectionately entitled, "An Angel...With Dirty Fingernails."

The image of Rev. Whynot taking her place at the altar brought back memories of another day in this same church. It was a happier day, filled with laughter and promise for a new beginning. Jane's wedding day, October 10, 1991. Rev. Whynot spoke on that day as well, about love and sharing another person's life.

Today, Rev. Whynot assumed her position and addressed the congregation in a comforting and soothing tone. It was almost as if she were addressing each one of us personally. Describing her presentation as a memorial meditation and tribute to Jane Hurshman-Corkum, she explained, "A memorial service is just that—a service in memory; remembering a special loved one and friend, a special child of God who has gone from our midst. I consider it a distinct honour and privilege that the family wanted me to be the one to help us remember their loved one: a wonderful person and a very special lady."

Reaching out to a grieving congregation, Rev. Whynot stressed that no one gathered at that church had a total picture of Jane Hurshman-Corkum, because no one person could know all of her, no matter how well or how long we might have known her. "Our memories are limited by a lack of continuity of both time and space. We all have our shared memories of the Jane the world knew—the courageous and outspoken activist; the survivor! But we also have our own personal and private memories of the Jane we alone knew. For her family, the memories are of a daughter and sister; for her sons, memories of their mother; for Joel, memories of a beloved wife and friend."

Pausing to control her emotion, Rev. Whynot continued. "Although the earthy part of Jane—the part that we could see and hear and touch and love—is gone from us now, her spirit lives on and will continue to live on through all the lives she touched in so many different ways. And we must work to make sure that her work does not die with her. Jane has passed on the torch to we who are left behind to grieve and to continue her good fight!"

Referring to the plight of abused women, she noted that she believed there could be no more fitting memorial to Jane's memory than to accept that torch she willingly and bravely carried. "We must carry it—all of us, both women and men alike—in her memory until the acceptance of the widespread abuse in our society is ended; until the justice system and public attitudes toward the abuse of women are changed to reflect the equality of sexes; until abusers find the help and courage they need to change their ways of relating; and until every victim of abuse is set free from their personal hell of pain, fear, self-blame, guilt and silence!"

Her voice quivering, Jane's friend continued the eulogy, pointing out that she felt certain all the good that Jane had done for so many people had more than redeemed her from her past in the eyes of God. "In a true sense, Jane laid down the last years of her life and carried her cross for others without counting the cost to herself, or complaining about the pain. And to some degree, I know so well just how much it must have cost her to live in the past so often."

For Rev. Whynot, this was a personal observation. It came from the heart and it came with meaning. "I will never forget the first time I shared a certain part of my own story in public. It was the most tense and draining experience you could ever imagine. When I was finished, I felt as if I had run a hundred-mile race non-stop. Some amount of telling is healing; some sharing is healthy, but her public audience kept calling on Jane over and over again to tell, to talk, to share, to give for the past eight or nine years. We kept her immersed in the past with all its pain and ugliness and she tried not to let us down. But by making her a larger-than-life hero and expecting her to be like that and act that way, we forgot that she was only human—a woman, a victim—with real needs."

Despite everything that Jane had done in recent years and the many people that she helped along the way, Rev. Whynot pointed out there are those who do not want to think of her as still being tortured by things in her past.

"We liked that brave mask she wore in public. There are those who don't like the idea of her being depressed in the midst of her new-found happiness, when everything seemed to be falling into place for her. Depression is a common human feeling. We are all acquainted with depression; many of us have experienced it ourselves. But," she continued, "by making Jane our larger-than-life hero, we didn't give her the time or the space to stop and forget the past for awhile or to just take time to concentrate on looking after her own needs, or to take time to cherish the beauty and the love and to smell the roses in her present life with those she loved and who loved her so dearly! You see, by asking so much of her, we were able to avoid our own responsibilities for speaking out to help make our society a better, safer place in which to live."

Rev. Margie Whynot and Jane Hurshman-Corkum had a very special relationship that she describes as being unique among all of her other friendships.

"Up until ten years ago, I knew of Jane—she was there on the periphery of my life—but I didn't really know her. We lived quite near each other geographically and our life partners were well acquainted; many of our experiences with those partners were similar. But I didn't really get to know her until after the death of Billy Stafford, until after my own divorce, and until we both began speaking out in public and sharing our experiences in order to help other victims."

To the members of the congregation, it was obvious that Rev. Whynot was speaking from the heart. "I believe I speak for many other victims when I point to the Jane of ten years ago and say, 'There, but for the grace of God, go I.' But not one of us can look at the hero Jane and make the same claim, because none of us have had the time, the energy, the drive, or the courage to come even close to filling her shoes when it comes to the work she did so unceasingly and unselfishly. Jane did not show any prejudice against other victims who would not or could not follow in her large footsteps; she allowed us to go on at our own pace and in our own way, as long as we did something."

Although the relationship between Jane and Rev. Whynot had its beginning in their common experiences as victims, their friendship grew over the years. "We rarely ever saw each other in person or talked on the telephone, but gradually we discovered we had built a friendship that was a mutual support and admiration society of two. I was so proud of her for how she was persevering and bravely struggling to overcome her past and for all the work she was doing for others."

Whenever Jane spoke at a conference or rally, Rev. Whynot said she believed Jane was speaking on behalf of herself and other victims of abuse. "My path in life diverged from Jane's and I chose the ordained ministry, or perhaps I should say God chose me. But I did choose a much quieter, low-key and much less public way of working with and for victims, and for the rights of all women in society. Our differing ways and levels of involvement did not cause tension in our friendship; if anything, it made it stronger and more special."

Rev. Whynot spoke of Jane as a deeply spiritual person with a strong faith and a great love for God, even though she was not a church person. "Others can also testify to just how much Jane's faith and spiritual meditations meant to her in her ongoing struggle for healing and wholeness. She was always so happy for even the most simple sharing of faith. But that's just the way she was toward a lot of people—always grateful for whatever help, moral support, gifts, or acts of love and kindness that came her way."

Turning to Jane's family who were assembled at the front of the church near the altar, Rev. Whynot attempted to soothe their sorrow with words of encouragement. To her sons, she said, "Allen, Jamie and Darren: she talked about you so often and she wanted so much for you to have good, peaceful, and productive lives. She gave thanks and was so proud of each of you for every little hill you climbed and for each type of turmoil you conquered. And she was so grateful for each little ray of sunshine, joy, laughter, and love you offered her."

To Jane's parents, Maurice and Gladys Hurshman; to her brother, Doug; and to her sisters, Mona and Sandra, Rev. Whynot expressed assurances that "you played a very important role in her life. I remember how you were here flocking around her and supporting her on her wedding day, making sure that her special day was even more special.

"Above all else, that which brought Jane the greatest sense of happiness in her life was finding Joel, and finding true love and happiness for the very first time in her life. I was absolutely thrilled to be able to be here last fall to help them celebrate the commitment of their love, to witness the happiness and realize what a wonderful future they had together. Joel, I grieve that your future was cut so short in such a tragic way, but I know from Jane's letters over the past year or so just how much you meant to her and that you were helping her to gather some beautiful memories to replace the ugly and painful ones of the past. You gave her joy; you gave her real happiness; you gave her real love. Don't ever doubt that.

"Neither her death nor our pain and grief, nor all our questions can ever take away from the beauty and goodness of what you gave her, Joel, and what the two of you shared in your too-short life together."

Then, drawing on her own inner strength, Rev. Whynot continued. "I will always think of Jane as my 'angel…with dirty fingernails.' Jane was my hero, but she was not perfect. No one is! She was a real and normal human person first; and being the real person that she was, she knew real pains and fears and more than her share of hurts; she knew tortured thoughts and depression was part of her life. She also had her faults and weaknesses just as the rest of us imperfect sinners do. Nevertheless, she was my hero."

Fondly recalling the good memories she had of her departed friend, Rev. Whynot noted, "Jane will continue to be my symbol of strength and courage. I will remember her as a warm, loving, compassionate person of faith. I'll remember her for her unselfish giving-until-it-hurts, and her willingness to share her dark side as well as her light. I'll remember her as being strong, brave, funny, kind, sincere and thoughtful. But, most of all, I'll remember her as my dear precious friend."

As a statement of comfort to the mourners, she concluded, "Jane is at rest; she has found peace at last."

Before the service ended, Jane's youngest sister, Mona Donnelly, who had come from her home in Barrie, Ontario, for the service, replaced Rev. Whynot at the altar. In words filled with emotion and sorrow, Mona delivered a message to the congregation on behalf of Jane's family.

Fighting back tears, she forced herself to speak. "Janey; How we loved and cared for you! How precious you were in our sight. We long to hold you again, to see your smile, and to hear you laugh. We miss you so already.

"Her death is a tragedy; a loss that we will carry with us always," Mona continued. "Jane was truly a symbol of hope to the abused people in our society. We want you to know that her death was not a defeat for them, but a rallying point. We vow to continue to work to create the society which Jane so desperately wanted—where the virtues of love and caring and respect for one another will supplant the evils of anger and hatred and violence.

"Jane was indeed a lady with a mission and one who touched the lives of many. So let us unite and continue on in her footsteps. We miss you so, and we will always cherish the memories that you have given us. May the very love of God envelope us all, that we might carry her banner until all the pain stops."

It was over. But the memories and the sadness would continue. No amount of comforting words or insightful recollections could replace the real thing.

Gone, But Not Forgotten

The Halifax City Police Department has wrapped up its investigation into the mysterious death of Jane Hurshman-Corkum by officially labelling it a suicide, but the final chapter in her story is still being written. In fact, the Cole Harbour RCMP has not yet concluded its probe into the death threats Jane had been receiving a month before her body was found on the Halifax waterfront. Family and friends are continuing to push for more answers, saying the police investigation was a whitewash.

But even with police assurance that an indepth and thorough investigation was conducted, the results of which they say confirm the suicide theory, family members and many friends remain certain that Jane would not take her own life. They say there is too much evidence to support the idea of a murder plot—the death threats, the locked car door, the location of the wound, the lack of a suicide note. Unfortunately, they contend the police investigators, in their haste to prove a suicide theory, carelessly overlooked or discounted pertinent and important clues that might have led to a different conclusion.

One person in particular, Jane's father Maurice Hurshman, says he will never accept the possibility that his daughter would take her own life. He says she had too much to live for and was not capable of suicide. Jane's mother Gladys shares the same beliefs, pointing out her daughter cared too much for her children to kill herself and leave them alone.

It will take a great deal of time for the emotional wounds left in the wake of Jane's death to heal. For the family of Jane Hurshman-Corkum, those scars will never go away. In the weeks following her death, Maurice asked questions about his daughter's death but says he received no satisfactory answers. In fact, he explains, the only information he was able to gain regarding the investigation was largely through media reports.

"They [the police] never told us anything about their investigation or what they were finding," he told me, and as insensitive as it sounds, he officially heard of his daughter's death on the radio while driving to Halifax on the morning of February 24, the day after her body was discovered. "They would not tell us very much, but I'll never believe she killed herself; I'll never believe it myself. She had too much to live for; she had no reason to do it."

If dealing with Jane's death and the speculation that she had committed suicide was not bad enough, the months following Jane's death became even more complicated when Gladys had to be hospitalized for surgery. She has recovered, and together Jane's parents are attempting to move forward with their lives.

They believe that this is the way their daughter would have wanted it. Yet, while they comfort and console each other, the pain is always there. While Maurice and Gladys try to rebuild their shattered lives and hope for answers to clear up some of the mystery surrounding Jane's death, all they are left with are memories of the good times they shared with their daughter.

Reliving these memories is painful, but they are also comforting, Maurice points out, since Jane spent much of her free time with them in their Danesville, Queens County home.

"Jane liked Halifax a lot," Maurice recalls, "but she also liked coming home for the weekends and the holidays. She liked to be with the family and enjoyed her free time. She did everything well and even when she was doing nothing, she was doing that well."

It is the long walks that he and his daughter used to take during these visits that he misses the most. "She loved to go for walks and go to the beaches." It was during those times that he had the opportunity to become acquainted with the real woman, the person that the world never had the chance to see. He knows some people are skeptical of the relationship he and his daughter developed after the trials in light of the kind of childhood she had, but he quickly notes that Jane had forgiven him for the things that had happened in the past.

"Janey always believed you shouldn't live in the past," Maurice observes, adding his daughter was a forgiving and understanding person. "She never had anything bad to say about anyone or anything. She really believed that if you couldn't say something good about somebody, then you shouldn't say anything at all." She also applied that same philosophy to the memory of Billy Stafford. "She really believed the past was the past and she wanted to leave it there. She didn't talk about him much at all."

However, Maurice does recall a few occasions in the years following the trials that Jane mentioned she had had nightmares about Billy Stafford and he accepts that as natural behaviour considering her past. "I don't think you could go through something like she went through and then forget it. I know she lived with it every day even after he died. I know she lived with the memories of Billy and what she finally had to do."

Instead of dwelling on her life with Billy Stafford, or talking about her life after Billy for that matter, he says Jane was more content to relish the good things that were happening in her life. "She always had good thoughts about people and things. She really loved her children. Those kids were everything to her; they were her life."

In the year-and-a-half prior to her death, Jane found a new kind of happiness with Joel Corkum. "It would be about two years this fall [1992] that I met Joel for the first time. Jane was really happy with him and everything seemed real good. She had a lot to live for."

Maurice admits he knew his daughter was having problems. He knew that she was in trouble with the law for shoplifting, but he points out, "She didn't talk about that because she didn't want us to worry about her. That shoplifting was something she couldn't control. It was a sickness because of all she went through, but I don't think it was enough to make her do that [commit suicide]."

Actually he was surprised police immediately assumed his daughter's death was a suicide. "I don't believe that it was. For one thing, she wasn't strong enough to do that to herself and for another thing, she had no reason."

Referring to the fact that Jane had nearly died in 1989 as the result of a pill overdose, he says, "We spent a lot of time together, just the two of us, and we talked a lot. She never mentioned suicide and I believe if she was thinking about that again, she would have said something to me.

I can't believe it was suicide and they will never be able to convince me that it was. If it was suicide, then there had to be someone else there to help her. If it was suicide, Jane would have left a suicide note. I know that."

He doesn't like the suggestions about the possibility that his daughter may have taken her own life because it makes him feel guilty that he failed her in some way. "If she was thinking about doing that, then I know I would have been able to get through to her. I would have stayed with her no matter how long it took to get her through that. It wasn't suicide."

Pulling a neatly folded piece of paper from his wallet, he produces what he believes is proof that Jane had no plans to kill herself. It is a note to her sick mother, Gladys. Jane had written it early Friday morning, February 21, while she was at work, just before her shift ended. Joel had hand-delivered it, along with some fabric Jane had purchased to make drapes, when he arrived in Danesville later that day.

The note read:

> *Dear mom,*
>
> *I am at work in the wee hours of the morning and thought I would drop you a few lines to say that I picked out this material for you and I hope you like it. I feel it will really brighten up your living room and if you want, I have the week of March Break off and I will come down for a couple of days to make them for you—maybe a different style—they will look real nice with sheers. I will make a couple of cushion covers and a doilie or two. It will look wonderful.*
>
> *Well I will talk to you on Sunday—till then take care and bye for now. Give dad my love and I will see you on Tues. the 25th for your doctor's appointment. I love you both.*
>
> *Janey XOXOXO*
> *XOXO*
> *XO*

"Does this sound like a person who is thinking about killing herself?" Maurice wonders, explaining that he believed his daughter had made these plans with the full intention of being alive after the weekend of February 21. Imagine his surprise and disbelief then early

Maurice Hurshman, Jane's father, believes this note confirms his daughter did not commit suicide.

on the morning of Saturday, February 22, when Maurice answered the phone to find his grandson Darren on the other end. He was calling from Halifax and he was looking for Joel, who had been staying overnight and the next day planned to do some car repairs for Jane's father.

The call came at about 1:15 a.m. He quickly summoned Joel to the phone and when he overheard him say, "I'll be right there," Maurice says he knew right away that something was wrong and that it involved his daughter. Joel was being called back to Halifax because Jane had failed to show up for her shift.

Only a week earlier, Maurice and Gladys had learned of the death threats Jane had been receiving since the beginning of the New Year. "Right away those threats came back to me and I knew something was wrong with Jane." As the days of the tragic weekend passed, Maurice's fears increased. "When I didn't hear anything by late Saturday, I knew it was bad and I told the wife to expect the worst because Janey had been gone too long."

When news finally came of Jane's death, it was devastating.

"I can't believe she's gone; I miss her so much. I know life will go on, but I will never forget her or the times we spent together. There won't ever be a day that goes by that I won't think about her."

Despite the difficulty he has accepting his daughter's death, he takes a great deal of comfort in the work that Jane had done in recent years. "She didn't talk much about that either, but I knew of the work she was doing. Jane liked life and I think it's a good thing that she could help someone else by sharing what she had gone through. She had so much to give and really wanted to help other people. She did help a lot of people through her work and I'll always remember that. We were all very proud of her."

In spite of all the publicity that surrounded his daughter during the trials and in the ensuing years after her ordeal became public knowledge, Maurice says the family never saw Jane as being anything other than just a member of the family. In fact, he credited Jane's ordeal for bringing them all closer together.

"She liked being with the family," he says. "She loved her work; she loved her family; she loved life and when she lived life, she enjoyed it to the fullest."

While Jane's parents openly expressed their feelings and thoughts about the loss of their daughter following her death, Joel, on the other hand, withdrew from the public light, avoiding the media's probing questions and suggestive rhetoric. In October 1991, Joel had openly stated his love for the woman he had taken as his bride. A man of few words, at the memorial service in February, he publicly declared his deep sense of loss and anger for having lost Jane only five months after they had set out to make a future with each other.

On April 7, less than two months after Jane's death, the CBC's *Fifth Estate* aired an interview with Joel Corkum in which he stated he had been aware of his wife's desperation and fear following receipt of the death threats earlier in the year. As well, he acknowledged that she had asked him to get her a gun for her own protection and that when he failed to fulfill her request, she got her own gun. When he asked how she had obtained it, she told him it would be better if he didn't know. He only saw the gun once.

While Jane's husband shied away from the public arena, her sister, Mona Donnelly, openly criticizes the police and their investigation, stating she is convinced the death was not a suicide. "I don't think that Jane committed suicide," she insists. "She was not a person to give up if something was wrong. After everything she went through for all those years, I can't see her committing suicide when she now had everything to live for."

Mona, who points out she had maintained close contact with her sister through the years, adds, "I never had any indication that she would do anything like that and if they say it was suicide, they'll have to have some really good proof to show me." Referring to the investigation, she expresses concern about the suicide speculation that began circulating almost immediately. "I'm not sure if they'll ever know what really happened that weekend, but I don't think people should be making these kinds of theories without proof to back them up."

In June when the Halifax City Police Department officially ruled Jane's death a suicide, Mona responded, reaffirming her dissatisfaction. "I'm very disappointed and saddened by the outcome of the investigation." Despite what evidence the police said they have, Mona insisted there are still many unanswered facts surrounding her sister's death.

"The public only knows a small part of our tragedy," she said. "You may be thinking that our family does not want to admit that Jane took her own life. Jane is dead; nothing will bring her back, I know that. I wish this was a clean-cut case, but it is not."

According to Mona, authorities have still not satisfied the family. "Police have not satisfied our questions. There are too many unanswered facts about what happened." Despite what police say their investigation uncovered, she pointed out, "Jane did not pull the trigger on herself. I believe with all my heart that, in time, the truth will be revealed."

Furthermore, she added that she believed the police have prematurely closed the file on her sister's death. "In my opinion, Jane's case should never have been treated as a suicide. On the contrary, it is an unsolved homicide." Acknowledging that Cole Harbour RCMP are continuing their probe, Mona continued, "I'm pleased to hear the RCMP are still investigating. Police must look beyond the obvious and I have faith that, eventually, all the answers will come out."

Perhaps, if any one feels the loss of Jane more than her father, husband or sister, it is her sons, Allen, Jamie and Darren. Before her death, Jane was confident her first born, Allen, would have a good life with a new wife and a good home. As well, she felt Jamie would find his way in life after graduating from high school in 1991. As for Darren, Jane had continued to worry about her youngest child because of the emotional scars he wore after the years of abuse he suffered as a child. After her death, he moved in with his grandparents in Danesville where he is sheltered and protected from public attention.

While the family of Jane Hurshman-Corkum is still rebounding from its loss, there are others who also suffer a void because of the death of a friend. Next to Jane's family, no one knew her suffering and emotional torment in the immediate years following the shooting of Billy Stafford better than her lawyer, Alan Ferrier.

In 1982, when the then-legal aid lawyer took on the case of Jane Hurshman, he had no idea of what was to come. Despite the fame that came her way, Jane was never free of emotional pain and following her death in February, Ferrier expressed remorse over the suffering she had endured.

"It's sad this kind of media circus surrounds her death as much as it surrounded her murder trial," he observed. "I don't think anyone can underestimate the kind of pain she endured before, during, and after her trial."

Pointing out that although he did not maintain contact with Jane in the years following her trial, he did talk with her occasionally. "Life didn't get better for her after the murder trials. She's always had a cloud over her head," he continued. "Some people's lives are destined to be tragic and she appeared to be one of those. It's sad she couldn't have lived her life with some sort of dignity without all the media hype."

Like Alan Ferrier, Brian Vallée, author of *Life With Billy*, said, following her death, that he was disturbed by the sudden loss of the woman he considered a close friend.

"I think that whatever happened will remain a mystery," he said. "There are more questions than answers." But Brian, who worked for CBC's *Fifth Estate* and met Jane during her trials, said he can accept what the police have determined was the cause of death.

"This woman suffered a lot of pain all her life," he observed. "There must have been emotional scars that would not be easy to deal with even though she tried to pull her life back together." He described Jane as "a caring and compassionate woman who worked hard to help others regardless of her own personal suffering. I don't think any one of us will ever know what sort of personal hell she was living in."

Following Jane's parole in April 1984, she befriended Wendy Annand, a parole officer with the Correctional Services of Canada. In the years that the two women knew each other, Wendy described Jane as a caring, thoughtful person who wanted to help other victims of abuse. "She wanted to give people an understanding of how a battered woman lives," she says. "Jane lived with the truth—it happened, she was a survivor and she wanted to make sure that no one else would suffer like that.

"Her legacy? She gave hope for many, many women. Anyone who ever heard her speak was touched by her sincerity and although she helped many people, Jane, the person I knew, never changed. Jane had a clear vision of the kind of world she wanted; one free of violence."

Jane Hurshman-Corkum was a survivor of some of the harshest abuse imaginable, yet she served as an example that there is a way out, Wendy explains. "She was a very humble, very private person, but I can tell you that Jane thought of herself as a survivor, not as a hero or celebrity." However, she adds, even though she felt she knew her friend very well, she finds it difficult to form an opinion about Jane's death. "I just don't know. There are too many unanswered questions."

But while some of Jane's family and friends have difficulty accepting that perhaps her death was, indeed, self-inflicted, others find that possibility very plausible. In the wake of her death, one of her closest friends in Halifax, Ann Keith, revealed that although she misses Jane, she does not discount the suicide theory. Ann revealed that, in fact, Jane had often talked with her about suicide, and said it was constantly on

Jane's mind. However, she would not speculate on the events of February 21, 1992. Instead, she would rather remember Jane as she knew her — "a close friend and caring person with a big heart; a person who wanted to ease the pain and suffering of others."

Ann, who is the executive director of Service for Sexual Assault Victims where Jane often did volunteer work, stressed she hoped Jane would be remembered for the good work she did and for the many people she helped. "We should let her rest in peace," she said. In the weeks following her friend's death, Ann acknowledged she had watched the police investigation very carefully and is satisfied they have done a thorough job.

"I accept their findings, I believe they have done everything they could." Furthermore, Ann says, she accepts the possibility that her friend may have committed suicide because, "We don't know the kind of pain Jane was suffering. For me personally, it is very sad to say that at this point I accept that she could have done it. What is important now is that we do not forget all the good work she did while she was alive."

Rev. Margie Whynot, like Ann Keith, said she too can accept the findings of the police investigation. "I was not at all surprised with the police report," she said, adding, "I thought from Day One that Jane had planned suicide. However, the one grey area that still remains is the death threats."

Both Rev. Whynot and Ann indicated they are encouraged by the fact the Cole Harbour RCMP are continuing to investigate that aspect of their friend's death.

Accepting the fact that her friend may have committed suicide may not be easy, Rev. Whynot says, "Jane was a person that did not want to let anyone down. Maybe she thought she would be letting down her friends, family, and all those women she has helped if they knew she had taken her own life."

That possibility may account for the lack of a suicide note, she suggested, while also recalling a number of specific arrangements that Jane had made prior to her death. Knowing these details—which included asking Rev. Whynot to give the eulogy at her funeral and making plans for Darren's care—helps Rev. Whynot to accept that, indeed, suicide was possible.

"Jane was still struggling with her past and with Billy's death," Rev.

Whynot says. "She was still a victim. In a way, Billy Stafford came back from the grave and made her a victim one last time."

Additionally, Rev. Whynot believes the timing of Jane's death was not coincidental. "It was no accident that Jane died almost ten years to the date of Billy's death."

"I think if it was suicide, it makes what she did for other women that much more special because of the suffering she went through," she explained. "She put aside her personal pain and suffering for many years to help others and they can never take away what she has done."

In fact, Rev. Whynot added, "It makes it so much more powerful that she died a violent death, regardless if it was murder or suicide. Her death has not changed my feelings toward her. I know how much Jane did for others despite her own inner struggle and to me that makes her even more a hero."

Now that the Halifax City Police have concluded their investigation, both Rev. Whynot and Ann Keith stressed that they believe the case should remain closed and there should be no enquiry unless new evidence surfaces.

Following Jane's death in February, public reaction was widespread and immediate.

One woman writing to *The Yarmouth Vanguard* said, "The first time I met and heard Jane Hurshman-Corkum speak was at a WHEN Conference in 1989, called Surviving Society's Violence. She again spoke of the horrible abuse in her past, the fact that abuse of that magnitude was still happening to so many others and that we must all fight to change attitudes in society about violence against women and children. There was no one in the audience, nor in any audience listening to Jane speak, that was left unmoved by or untouched by her words.... Through a mutual friend, I became acquainted with Jane. The woman I met was warm, open, and welcoming. She had a great sense of humour and a twinkle in her beautiful eyes. She was excited about her career, her life."

Another letter-writer to the *Daily News* in Halifax said, "It is with great sorrow I write this letter. The passing of Jane Hurshman-Corkum is a great loss to the Halifax-Dartmouth community. I heard Jane speak on three occasions. All her speeches were well-received. She did community work and helped many battered wives. It is sad that she did not reach out when she was in need. We women of abuse must be cautious in the future so we don't over-extend ourselves. It is important that we help, but not at our expense."

She continued, "Jane is at peace now and is resting with her higher power. Her husband and sons should be very proud of the work she accomplished. We survivors of abuse draw strength from the courage Jane showed. When dealing with any threats, we must inform the police so we can be protected. There are many out in the world that want us to be silent. We cannot let them win."

Epilogue

On June 8, following a three-month investigation, Halifax City Police concluded that the death of Jane Hurshman-Corkum was a suicide.

Staff Sgt. Don Thomander of the metro area police department said, "After reviewing all the evidence compiled by ourselves and the RCMP Cole Harbour detachment, no signs of foul play were uncovered." Forensic tests also failed to provide any evidence that the woman was murdered.

Staff Sgt. Thomander confirmed that after an extensive investigation involving the interview of more than sixty persons, authorities were ruling the cause of death to be suicide. "The medical examiner's office is in full agreement with our determination," he explained. "Indications are that sometime between 9 p.m. on February 21 and 9 a.m. on February 22, she killed herself." Her body was discovered at around 3:15 p.m. the next day, February 23.

Prior to her death, Jane had received a series of written and taped threats telling her to "shut up or be shut up." Although Halifax police have now concluded their investigation, Cole Harbour RCMP are still probing these mysterious threats and say they are awaiting the results of important tests before confirming any facts. However, sources with the Halifax Police say that even though authorities say a thorough and in-depth investigation was carried out, it was suspected from the outset that these were part of Jane's plan to commit suicide.

Staff Sgt. Thomander pointed out the pertinent facts that were discovered during their investigation—a .38 calibre handgun with no serial number and a bullet were found in the car. Forensic tests found residue on Jane's hands and on a blanket, which police said was used to muffle the gun when it was fired. Additionally, police said in their opinion her body had not been moved and there were no signs of a struggle or footprints around the vehicle. They know Jane had a similar weapon in her possession prior to her death, but they do not know it was the same one found in the car and admitted it is impossible to confirm whether it was the same one that fired the fatal bullet.

"We may never know where she obtained the gun that killed her," he added.

Now that the Halifax City Police have concluded their investigation, family and friends of Jane Hurshman-Corkum are hoping the RCMP will be able to shed some light on the mysterious circumstances surrounding the past few months of her life as well as the events as they unfolded on the weekend of February 21. In particular, it is commonly believed that if the RCMP can uncover the truth regarding the death threats, then more concrete facts will be known about her death.

RCMP Sergeant Gary Grant, the former media relations officer for the Province of Nova Scotia, agreed that learning the truth about the death threats is vital to gaining a better understanding about the death of Jane Hurshman-Corkum. Unfortunately, in June he indicated it could be between six months and a year before the results of forensic tests are known. Presently, evidence that was seized during the initial investigation—including answering machine tapes and stencils taken from Jane's Cole Harbour home after her death—are at the RCMP crime labs in Ottawa where they are undergoing a series of forensic tests.

However, Grant cautioned, "It could take months before we hear back from them." Frankly, he explained, because the file on Jane's death has already been closed by one police force, the results of these RCMP tests are no longer as urgent as they would be for an ongoing case. "You have to understand how these things work. These types of tests are done on a priority basis which means that those connected with more pressing cases are done first. Any ongoing investigation with suspects would take priority over this type of case. It's unfortunate, but that's how it works because the nature of this matter is such that the outcome of these tests will not affect the subsequent investigation."

Although Grant said he could not disclose specific details of the RCMP investigation into the death threats or the type of analysis being conducted in Ottawa, he said there would be some DNA testing on the notes that Jane had received as well as some voice print examinations from the tapes. As to the theory that Jane had sent herself the threats as part of an elaborate scheme to make her suicide look like a murder, Grant said only that it is not the policy of the RCMP to publicly discuss an ongoing investigation until facts are known.

"All I can say at this time is that our investigators are keeping an open mind," he added.

But for family and friends, it is difficult to remain impartial because they believe the origin of the mysterious death threats will provide the answers which they are seeking. For these people, the waiting continues long after Jane Hurshman-Corkum's tragic death.

Halifax police investigator Cpt. Jim Griffin dusts Jane's vehicle for fingerprints, searching for evidence of a possible murder suspect.

The Memories Remain

Although the sudden and tragic death of Jane Hurshman-Corkum left an indelible mark on the lives of those she touched, they still have the memories of a woman who survived unimaginable odds to become a symbol of hope and strength for many victims of abuse. Jane liked to express herself in poetry and the two poems that follow are hers. They are presented in dedication of her memory.

Time To Forget

The things we should remember are so easy to forget,
While occupied with work or play or fears that make us fret.
But things that now are past and gone and should be left behind,
Are those that constantly return to haunt the unconscious mind.
Especially the wrong or hurt we suffered long ago,
Which at the time appeared to be a devastating blow.
We told the guilty party we forgave the unkind act,
And yet that pardon never has become an actual fact.
Forgiving means forgetting and the heart is not sincere,
Unless the past is wiped out in friendly atmosphere.

At Peace

The ocean gives me peace,
The wind gives me energy,
The sun warms my spirit,
The flowers show me life,
And you, my friend, have given me support, caring,
understanding and friendship.
*   And I humbly say thank you.*

This bottle of flowers was found in the Halifax parking lot where police located Jane's body. The note reads, "In remembrance of Jane. The pain has to stop! We can be silent no longer," and is signed, "A man who never knew you (unfortunately)."

Appendix I:
the Cycle of Violence

In Canada, it is estimated that one out of every two men who beat their wives and children were themselves abused as children or witnessed violence in their home. Bob, a middle-aged man living in Nova Scotia, is a self-confessed child abuser and wife batterer. Today, he readily admits his nightmares began at a very young age but they continue to haunt him more than forty years later.

"I think it started on the day I was born," he reflects. Although he has difficulty remembering his early childhood, he has vivid memories from the time he was seven and of the painful years that followed.

"I really don't remember what happened in those years before that," he continues. "I guess maybe they were so painful that I blocked them out. There must be some reason that I can't remember anything that happened before I was seven. But I can tell you that I hate my father because of what he did to me and the others."

Bob was a member of a relatively large family with a number of brothers and sisters. While they may have seemed normal from the outside, he says, matter-of-factly and without hesitation, that his father physically abused them all, particularly their mother.

Although authorities admit the rate of child sexual abuse appears to be growing at alarming proportions, they stress non-sexual physical abuse also poses a very serious threat to the young people of today's society. It is not the visible bruises or broken bones that will have an impact on these physically abused children for the rest of their lives but rather the emotional scars that will determine future behaviour. It is this learned behaviour that continues the cycle of violence.

"There was no sexual abuse in our home," Bob points out quickly. "I guess maybe he thought that was too disgusting or something. But he did like to hit us a lot and most of the time for no good reason." Because Bob grew up thinking that physical force was the acceptable norm in the family unit, he too became a child abuser and wife batterer when he had his own family. "I thought it was alright to do those things because our father used to do it all the time." Today, Bob admits that he, like his father before him, used physical violence to cope in his family setting.

"I know I can't really blame him for what I do now, but I think that maybe he has something to do with it," Bob reasons. Mental health professionals and authorities agree the cycle of violence begins with a dysfunctional family and permeates through each generation on a continuing basis until that chain is broken. Based on a growing list of statistics, it is commonly agreed that most abusers have themselves been abused as children.

Bob agrees with that observation and says he is proof of that reality. "It's not that I enjoy doing the things I do. It's just that I saw how my father dealt with his problems for all those years." Hitting, slapping, yelling, punching, and kicking were all normal actions in his home when he was growing up. "I didn't know you could deal with your problems any other way."

There were numerous occasions, Bob recalls, that he would have to go to school with bruises on his body because his father had vented his frustration by beating up on him. "But I didn't get the worst," he says, adding that no one could escape his father's anger or his fists, and alludes to one incident when his father hit one of his brothers so hard that he knocked him down a set of stairs, breaking his arm in the process.

"I remember one time when he punched one of my sisters in the mouth so hard that he knocked out three teeth," he says. "Then there was the time he cracked two of her ribs when he kicked her." Bob also says he watched helplessly on numerous occasions as his father "beat up" his mother. "It happened so many times that they all sort of run together," Bob suggests. "He would be just hitting her all the time, it seemed. He'd hit her around the head and punch her in the stomach almost every day and sometimes right out the blue. It got so bad in the end that she didn't even cry anymore. It was almost like she had become his puppet and he was pulling her strings."

But despite all the violence in Bob's childhood home, he says he and the other children were forbidden to talk to anyone about how they sustained their injuries. "We became really good liars. I think maybe our teachers suspected something was going on but that was more than thirty-five years ago and back then people didn't talk about child abuse like they do today."

Bob describes his childhood years as "pure hell. I couldn't wait until I was old enough to leave home and get out on my own where I could get away from him," he says.

"I swore that if I ever had kids, I would not do to my family what he did to us." He admits now that he could not keep that personal promise. "It's a terrible thing that I do," he realizes. "But it's like I can't control myself. I've become just like my father and I hate myself."

Although Bob has no formal education beyond high school, he did manage to create a comfortable lifestyle which he enjoyed with his wife and two children for a number of years. "We didn't have a lot of money to spare but we did manage to get by for awhile," he explains. However, as the years went by and money difficulties kept growing, Bob confesses, "I eventually lost it."

He recalls, "It started one night when my wife was trying to figure out what bills we were going to pay. She just kept saying over and over that we didn't have enough money to make all the payments and I just snapped. It was like someone else had control of me and I hit her. I slapped her right side of the head."

Bob stresses he regretted that first act of violence and felt so ashamed that he pulled back from his family. But as the family's monetary situation grew worse, he continued to lose control of his temper on a more regular basis. He lashed out more frequently at his family until the acts of violence became a normal reflex. "I'll never forget the first time I hit one of my kids," he notes. "It was like I could see myself hitting him, but it didn't seem like it was me. When I saw him crying because of what I had done, it brought back all those memories of what my father had done to me and I swore I'd never do it again." But the violence continued.

It persists even now, he admits, although he accepts the fact that he has to find help. "I know it has to stop," he agrees. "I know I can't keep doing this. I think I've already caused enough damage to my family. I know I've hurt them bad and I hate myself for what I've done."

Most health care professionals agree that while abusers are reluctant to talk about their pasts and their actions, communication is the best weapon against domestic violence. Abusers can be helped but society must first learn that the crisis is real.

In recent years, the government of Nova Scotia has finally started addressing the reality of the problem. For instance, in May 1991, the provincial government introduced a series of new initiatives that includes the establishment of a provincial coordinator's office with its mandate to focus on prevention, education, and coordination. Personnel at this new office will develop public education strategies, identify training programs for community professionals, coordinate research activities into family violence, and promote the exchange of information between government departments and community-based agencies.

By looking at one Nova Scotia municipality in isolation, we can see the need is real and these types of initiatives are a step in the right direction. Liverpool RCMP say the number of assault charges laid in Queens County in 1990 show a very serious trend. That year, there were sixty-seven local charges of assault of which thirty were spousal-related.

In conjunction with the new coordinator's office, the province also put in place in 1991 assistance for therapeutic services for batterers and a spousal homicide study which is presently underway. Providing assistance for batterers is the right approach to prevention. In order to reduce the reoccurrence of spousal assault and to give new hope to families that have been victimized by violence in the home, it's the perpetrator who needs help.

Through these types of programs, it can only be hoped that a concentrated effort on changing attitudes through public education will make a difference in the lives of many Nova Scotia families.

Debi Forsyth-Smith, president of the Nova Scotia Advisory Council on the Status of Women, recently said, "Violence against women is unacceptable and its elimination is the responsibility of the entire community." However, she added, violence will only be eradicated through major social change. That change must start now.

Appendix II

Nova Scotia Transition Houses
Transition houses provide emergency shelters for
women and children who are being victimized at home.

Amherst
Cumberland Co. Transition House
Business 667-1344
Crisis/Helpline **667-1200**

Antigonish
Naomi Society
Business 863-3807
Crisis/Helpline **863-2852**

Bridgewater
Harbour House
Business 543-3665
Crisis/Helpline **543-3999**

Halifax
Bryony House
Business 423-7183
Crisis/Helpline **422-7650**

Kentville
Chrysalis House
Business 679-6544
Crisis/Helpline **582-7877**

New Glasgow
Tearmann Society
Business 752-1633
Crisis/Helpline **752-0132**

Port Hawkesbury
Leeside Society
Business 625-1990
Crisis/Helpline **625-2444**

Sydney
Cape Breton Transition House
Business and
Crisis/Helpline **539-2945**

Truro
Third Place Transition House
Business 893-4844
Crisis/Helpline **893-3232**

Yarmouth
Juniper House
Business 742-4473
Crisis/Helpline **742-8689**

Women's Centres in Nova Scotia

Women's centres offer support, referrals for counselling,
and print resources on a wide variety of women's issues.

Antigonish

Antigonish Women's Resource
Centre
219 Main Street
Antigonish 863-6221

Bridgewater

Second Story Women's Centre
99 York Street
Bridgewater 543-1315

New Glasgow

Pictou County Women's Centre
6th Floor, Maritime Building
New Glasgow 755-4647

North Sydney

Northside Women's Centre
308 Rear Commercial Street
North Sydney 794-8666

Sheet Harbour

L.E.A. Place
Eastern Shore Learning
Opportunities for Women
Sheet Harbour 885-2668

Sydney

Everywoman's Centre
436 George Streeet
Sydney 567-1212

Wolfville

Acadia University Women's
Centre
Room 504, Resource Centre
Student Union Building
Acadia University
Wolfville, N.S. B0P 1X0
542-2287 ext. 140